CREATING FOUR-PART HARMONY

Effective Ideas
for Ministers of Music

by

Lois and Fred Bock

Hope Publishing Company
CAROL STREAM, IL 60188

Cover design by Timothy Botts

To

Dr. and Mrs. Charles C. Hirt

This book is lovingly dedicated to you,
Charles and Lucy, because your dreams
are our legacy. You are mentors who
are our encouragers and counselors
who are our friends.

CONTENTS

FOREWORD — Dr. Lloyd John Ogilvie 7

INTRODUCTION 11

CHAPTER 1 — HARMONY WITH GOD 18
        The Foundation for Our Work

CHAPTER 2 — HARMONY IN THE CHURCH 34
        Part 1 — Harmony with the Congregation
        Part 2 — Harmony with the Volunteers
        Part 3 — Harmony with the Staff
        Part 4 — Harmony with the Senior Minister

CHAPTER 3 — HARMONY WITH THE CHOIR 73
        Part 1 — Turning a Choir Into a Family
        Part 2 — The Outreach of the Choir
        Part 3 — What to Do Prior to the Choir Season
        Part 4 — What to Do Prior to Every Rehearsal
        Part 5 — Running a Smooth Rehearsal
        Part 6 — What to Do Before the Next Rehearsal
        Part 7 — "The Best Laid Plans . . . "

CHAPTER 4 — HARMONY IN YOUR OWN FAMILY
. . . . 123
        Keeping Personal Relationships in Tune

CODA — A Musical P.S. 138

BONUS SECTION — 147
        How to Make Your Choir Sound Better — FAST!
        Fred's 101 Favorite Anthems
        Suggested Inspirational Reading
        "The Church Musician and The Copyright Law"

RESOURCE MATERIALS — 168
        Choir By-laws
        Retreat Schedule
        Sample Bulletins of Worship Services

ACKNOWLEDGEMENTS

We are thankful for the help and assistance of several people:

David Hempstead, who patiently taught two before-the-computer-age, non-mechanical friends to get every word of this book on a word processor.

Barbara Heimburger and Sally Jordan, who carefully rubricated our manuscripts and matched plural and singular verb tenses with plural and singular nouns and pronouns.

To the Cathedral Choir of the First Presbyterian Church of Hollywood for allowing us the privilege of being your leaders.

To Dr. Lloyd John Ogilivie and the entire staff at the First Presbyterian Church of Hollywood for the rich and rewarding experience of being on your "team."

To our sons, Stephen and Jonathan, for allowing us to experience four-part harmony at home. Our lives are richer because you have given us colorful chords, accelerated tempos, and love.

FOREWORD

The purpose of the church and worship is no less than what the Westminster Catechism declares to be the chief end of humankind. It is to glorify God and enjoy Him forever.

Paul concludes his prayer for the Christians in Asia Minor recorded in Ephesians 3:14-21 with a doxology that defines this purpose: "To Him (God) be glory in the church by Christ Jesus throughout all ages, world without end. Amen" (Eph. 3:21, parenthesis added).

The reigning Christ is in His church to glorify the Father through us. Glory means both manifestation and adoration. We behold glory and we give glory, and Christ enables us to do both. He is God's manifestation with us and in us, and the one who motivates our praise. The Lord of the church is at the same time the glory of God in the church and the glorifier of God through the church.

Churches, like individuals, become what they envision. This is especially true for how we picture what can happen in our worship services. Christ is in our midst to glorify the Father through every aspect of the service. Everything from the prelude to the postlude is to be Christ-inspired and Christ-guided. He glorifies the Father as we sing praise. Confession means "to say after." We allow Christ to help us confess anything that stands between us and the Father and between us and any other person. He also guides our confession of our sins of omission in accepting the power and greatness, He wills for the ministry of every Christian. Thanksgiving breaks forth as we claim our forgiveness through the cross.

Then Christ guides us in prayers of intercession for others and supplication for specific situations of need. He gives us the boldness to pray for what the Father is more ready to give than, often, we are to ask. Christ helps us know how and what to pray about the things we have committed to Him. We pray in the presence and power of His Name, the Name that reaches the Father's heart and conquers the forces of evil.

And Christ is the inspiration of the exposition of the Word. All Scripture leads to Him, Calvary, and the new life He gives us with the Father. In preaching, we respond to the plea, "Sir, we wish to see Jesus" (John 12:21). Richard Baxter's reminder must always be before the preacher, "I preach as a dying man to dying men and women as if never to preach again."

The central theme of the sermon provides the basis of the planning of the entire worship order.

At the conclusion of Christ's glorification of the Father the people are called to dedication. The worship in the sanctuary ends and our service as disciples in the world begins. The people are commissioned as ministers of Christ for the ministry of personal evangelism and mission in society.

Worship led by Christ the Glorifier of the Father requires the four-part harmony Fred and Lois Bock describe so effectively in this book. Christ is the cantus firmus of the music for the worship of the First Presbyterian Church of Hollywood with every anthem, response, hymn, solo, or musical group blending in polyphonic glorification. That is possible because of the close working relationship by the Director of Music, Pastor, Organist, Choir and Congregation.

Each summer, after I have outlined the themes of messages for the program year, Dr. Bock selects the anthems and responses, hymns and solos, and together we seek the guidance of Christ the Glorifier in the development of each order of worship. Weekly meetings with the organist and others giving leadership in the services further defines the vision for the forthcoming Sunday.

Fred Bock's commitment to excellence is expressed in his planning for the music to heighten each aspect of the flow of Christ's glorification of the Father in our worship services. Stunning classical and contemporary anthems stimulate our people's minds and stir their hearts. Sensitive choral and congregational responses deepen our praise, confession, thanksgiving, intercession, supplication and dedication. The Glorifier has a ready and open channel in Fred Bock to lead a singing church in joyous praise.

Dr. Bock has enabled our choirs to claim their calling in the leadership of worship. His emphasis in communication rather than presentation has given the choirs dynamic verve and vitality.

I am delighted that Fred and Lois have written this book together. They both are leaders in the development of worship and devotional music and literature for the contemporary church. And together, they have led our Cathedral Choir in being a family of faith, a church in miniature, a praying band of spiritual adventurers and a caring community.

What Fred and Lois Bock have written in this book is authentic. They live what they believe. And their vision for a music program of a church today is happening in our congregation because of them.

I like the way Fred expresses the continuing need for innovation and freshness. "Let's not bore people with sameness or predictability, but make them expectant of new ways of praising God." This book is a call to four-part harmony for musical glory in the church. It is a delight to commend it to you for your ministry of glorifying God and enjoying Him forever . . . and together!

Lloyd John Ogilvie

INTRODUCTION

Can you picture it? Richard II, the beleaguered English King, paces back and forth in his dark, damp prison cell, awaiting his execution. He contemplates his imminent death, while verbally reviewing the circumstances and people who are responsible for this dastardly sentence. In the midst of his musing, he hears music in the distance:

> How sour sweet music is
> When time is broke and no proportion kept!
> So is it in the music of men's lives.
> >William Shakespeare
> >*Richard II*

The poetic wisdom of Shakespeare, who penned these words almost 400 years ago, certainly applies to directors of music as we approach the twenty-first century. The sweet music of our lives can easily turn sour if our priorities and "proportions" are not kept in order. In all probability we would never find ourselves pacing back and forth in a prison cell because of our lack of "priority," but we might find ourselves in a prison of our own making. The walls can be sloppily constructed of bricks of disorganization, lack of direction, an over-crowded schedule, the inability to work with others, stagnant complacency, and lost spiritual purpose.

FRED: Since my teenage years I have had the privilege of being involved in the world of church music. I started by playing the piano for the evening services at my church in New York. In the years since that formidable age, I have been given many opportunities to expand my experiences and sharpen my musical skills. I have learned a great deal from people I work for, people I work with, people who work for me, choir members, pastors, my church, fellow music directors, other music publishers, as well as my own family. When my various careers seem to overlap at a frantic pace I often ask myself, "Why am I doing this? Wouldn't it be easier just to sit quietly in some ivory tower more tranquil and less populated than Los Angeles, and only write my music?" Inevitably, the answer to my question is that I have been placed in this position to affect people's lives with music and by so doing, draw them closer to God. There can be no greater reward in life! Because I feel called by God I continue to wear my many hats. Over twenty-five years ago, my wife, Lois, joined in this pursuit. Together, we have raised a family, served in churches, established friendships, traveled thousands of miles and met a multitude of people. We have shared success and failure, and have grown as a team, and as individuals.

LOIS: As a child, I also, sat on a piano bench practicing scales and chords. But my early lessons did not take hold of me as they did Fred. I can still play "Here We Go, Up a Row, to a Birthday Party," from John Thompson's first book; if asked, I can even play a C Major chord. With so little musical training and such lack of knowledge, of course, I thought there would be no place in the church music world for me. How wrong I was! Soon after we were married, I learned that Fred's career involved people as much as music. I feel called to be a helper in people's lives. Together Fred and I have learned that there are many ways to help others: listening, encouraging, directing, entertaining, praying, counseling, and even giving financial and career advice. We have learned to be friends to all kinds of people with all kinds of lifestyles. I spend many hours each week helping Fred do his church work. This part of his career has truly been a rewarding experience for me and I have enjoyed our shared calling.

We have grown through the difficult periods as much as through the glorious ones, probably even more so. There have been times that we have had to swallow our pride, admit our mistakes, make amends and apologies and go on — even if we didn't feel like it. We have learned valuable lessons often at times when our own enthusiasm waned. Then the "still small voice" gently reminded us that, "My grace is sufficient for you, for my power is made perfect in weakness. . . . I delight in weaknesses, in difficulties. For when I am weak, then I am strong." (II Corinthians 12:9-10)

Church work is not always a "mountain-top" experience. That's a myth! Rather, it is while in the valleys that personal growth and dependency upon God are developed. During our visits to workshops, concerts, conventions, churches and campuses, we have met pastors, directors of music and their families, choir members, students striving to enter the music world, and members of assorted congregations. That list probably includes some of you who are now reading our words. Over the years many of you have expressed your dreams and disappointments, your successes and failures, your arguments and misunderstandings with pastors, co-workers, and choir members. We have come to understand personally the frustrations of a family member with little time to spend at home. Now we want to share our thoughts and experiences with you. We do this with a sense of vulnerability. Surely we have not done everything perfectly. Our mistakes have included wrong attitudes and topsy-turvy priorities. At times, we have even permitted our motives to become self-serving. As you can see, we also are in the process of learning and growing. As fellow travelers on the road to musical and relational excellence, we offer our ideas and visions for your examination.

It has always seemed a strange irony to us that the very department within the church which can produce such gorgeous musical harmonies often provides the soil where discord is planted and nurtured. It was a freeing discovery for us when we found out that it doesn't have to be that way! People can actually work and sing together and still be friends.

FRED: I hate to admit it, but we directors of music are often the cause of this problem. It's true that we sometimes possess the biggest and yet the most fragile of egos. However, I believe our egos can be tempered to a healthy normal if we will recognize the Source and Giver of our talents and remember the reason for our ministry.

If we mistakenly see ourselves as "stars" then we will probably develop ugly habits of demanding our own way and insisting on taking the center stage. We have come to understand that there is no place within the church structure for "stars" if we sincerely desire to honor and glorify God. Giving God His rightful place in our work will indeed bring harmony into our lives and into our ministry. If we see ourselves as part of the team called by God to help others understand and praise Him, then our goal in life will not be the applause we receive for a performance well done, but rather, an eternal "Well done, thou good and faithful servant."[1] We are indeed invited to a privileged station in life — that of guiding members of our congregation to a place where they can worship God, be healed of hurts, be forgiven, and actually encounter Jesus Christ. That is worth a great deal more than mere applause, which quickly evaporates and vanishes.

Do you think of harmony as applying only to music? Not so! Harmony has a place in the natural world: the beauty of seasons, the unity of relationships, the balance of art and architecture, and the order of business. Harmony is never in the singular; it is always plural. In the music world, harmony is not created with only a soloist, a single melody line, or one note. It takes voices and notes sung or played together to produce true harmony. Life is that way as well. Relational harmony is not necessary if we live as emotional soloists or hermits, never seeing, talking to, or working with other people. In the music world we often speak of "four-part harmony," therefore, we have loosely organized our thoughts into a "four-part" outline:

---

1   Matthew 25:21

1. Harmony with God.
2. Harmony in the Church (pastors, staff, and congregation)
3. Harmony with the Choir
4. Harmony in your own Family (married or single)

Is that possible? Not with a hundred per cent of the people, a hundred per cent of the time! But we can try, can't we?

We know it can work if we and our fellow strugglers are in philosophical agreement as to the purpose of our music careers and endeavors.

FRED: Music has been my vocation and avocation for as long as I can remember. My mother tells me that I was about five years old when I started playing whatever songs I heard at school on the piano. Not only was it enjoyable to play, but I also liked the attention I got when I entertained relatives and friends of the Bock family. My parents knew that I needed to be reminded that I was only a part of the whole and not even the center of the whole! I had to live within the structure of a harmonious family. Through their repeated reminders I learned that my talents were God-given and that I should honor Him with my music. I have also come to learn that my talents in music are no greater than those He has given others in art, business, humor, hospitality, law, medicine, teaching, landscaping and many, many other fields. I am grateful for that early training, and I do try to remember that lesson each day.

Within the body of our local churches and within the walls of our homes, we are instructed to live in peace — that means to live in harmony! We do so by holding each other accountable for our actions, by striving to resolve discord, by encouraging individual growth and expansion, and by loving and accepting each other as imperfect human beings. Learning to put four-part harmony into practice is an ongoing challenge which requires a great deal of practice and rehearsal.

We hope that in a small way we can do this for you, not only in your work, but also in your relationships with other people. We would like to inspire you to a renewed dedication to serve God with your talents. May full, rich, harmony resound in every area of your life.

Chapter 1

HARMONY WITH GOD

The foundation for our work

HARMONY WITH GOD

> The true purpose of our existence in this world ... is quite simply, to look for God, and, in looking, to find Him: and, having found Him, to love Him, thereby establishing a harmonious relationship with His purposes for His creation.
>
> Malcolm Muggeridge
> *A Twentieth Century Testimony* [1]

Living in relationship with God is the primary harmony in life. This harmonious relationship has been initiated by God Himself. II Corinthians 6:16 tells us:

> We are the temple of the living God. As God has said: "I will live with them and walk among them, and I will be their God, and they will be My people."

Yet, even though we are His people, that doesn't mean life will always be easy. In fact, it might seem that life is never easy! But life can have meaningful fulfillment and happiness when it is built on a foundation that is secure in a relationship of harmony with God. Our days can be lived in accord with the Creator of life, of music, of beauty, of love, and of worship.

---

1   New York, Thomas Nelson, 1978

Men and women in church ministry are especially vulnerable to spiritual, emotional, and physical burnout. Why? Because most of these "servants" are trying to balance an unrealistic schedule of constant demands of people (including their own families), the weekly grind of performance (for lack of a better word) and programming, and to stretch every dollar at home and at work, with too little money. Every music director in the country seems to be either underpaid or not paid at all. Striving to be a spiritual leader when the fuel tank is riding on "E" is another reason for burnout, as is trying more to please people instead of God.

At a time like this, indulging ourselves in self-pity is easy. We feed that heavy, uncomfortable feeling of lack of appreciation. Let's face it, we all like to feel that what we do is worthwhile and valued, and there is probably nothing wrong with that need as long as it is not our sole motivation. If it hampers our work, dampens our feelings of self worth, and puts a shadow across the face of our faith, then we need to allow God's healing light to expose it and rebalance our emotions.

Stress and tension, two of the biggest contributors to burnout, are also caused by taking on the load of responsibility that rightfully belongs to God alone. He doesn't intend to have us pace the floor at night carrying a weight that only He can shoulder.

And how do we, Lois and Fred, know all this? Because we've been there! Now the question is: how do we overcome and protect ourselves from this very common malady? Just as there are many causes for the affliction, so there are many cures. There isn't one simple pat answer.

One of the most basic reasons for the depletion of spiritual energy is our failure to schedule God into our twenty-four hour day. Sometimes we put our relationship with God on hold while we pour ourselves into our work, friendships, financial planning, education, the quest for "the better things of life," and even our "call" to the music ministry. Whenever we find ourselves doing this, we also find our lives full of worry and stress. We have been guilty of leaving God out of our daily lives . . . the sin of omission. We do not do this consciously, it just seems that He has been quietly relegated to a lesser position in our lives.

On January 25th of this year, we were again taught the lesson from Oswald Chambers' daily devotional book, *My Utmost For His Highest*:

> "But when it pleased God...." Gal. 1:15

> As workers for God we have to learn to make room for God — to give God "elbow room." We calculate and estimate, and say that this and that will happen, and we forget to make room for God to come in as He chooses. Would we be surprised if God came into our meeting or into our preaching in a way we had never looked for Him to come? Do not look for God to come in any particular way, but look for Him. That is the way to make room for Him. Expect Him to come, but do not expect Him only in a certain way. However much we may know God, the great lesson to learn is that at any minute He may break in. We are apt to overlook this element of surprise, yet God never works in any other

> way. All of a sudden God meets the life —
> "When it was the good pleasure of God . . . ."
>
> Keep your life so constant in its contact
> with God that His surprising power may
> break out on the right hand and on the left.
> Always be in a state of expectancy, and see
> that you leave room for God to come in as He
> likes.[2]

Don't you ever find life complicated and confusing? Of course! And yet because of our common human weakness and foolishness, we neglect the Source of renewal, truth and order. Here are some of the steps we can take to right this important relationship immediately and effectively.

Matthew 6:33 continually reminds us of the order we are to keep in our lives:

> But seek first His kingdom and His righteousness, and all these things will be given unto you as well.

Could it be that "all these things" might mean more inspiration, more stamina for the job, and more creativity?

Initiate the discipline of giving God some time each day. Recently a young teenager, who shares our home and same last name, asked, "What does *tête-à-tête* mean?" Our high school French came in handy because we could quickly answer with "one-on-one conversation," "head-to-head," "eyeball-to-eyeball," or "private talk."

---

2   New York, Dodd, Mead & Co., 1935

Maybe what we should ask God to do for us is to give us a desire for a *tête-à-tête* with Him. The first step is to make the decision to schedule the time and faithfully keep that divine appointment with Him.

Wonderful sermons have been preached on the subject of having consistent daily devotions with God. Many a helpful book has been written to guide our thoughts into a deeper communion with Him. From time to time, blow the dust off those books and get back on schedule. One helpful tool that we use for our own self-discipline is the keeping of a prayer journal. Several years ago we purchased *My Personal Prayer Diary* by Catherine Marshall and her husband, Leonard LeSourd;[3] we found journaling to be a valuable springboard to a more systematic devotional life. Not only did it give us a written record of our prayer requests, but it also gave us the added benefit of seeing God's care of our own personal needs as well as His repeated answers. This became our very own spiritual history book, a kind of diary. When we are desperately in need of His help and guidance, we thumb through page after page of prayer requests and see subsequent answers to these prayers. It's an encouragement to see recorded *right there in black and white,* that He has been faithful to us in the past. He is indeed worthy of our trust today and capable of handling whatever we bring to Him.

Have you ever noticed that when you consistently make the effort to keep an appointed hour with the Lord, He does indeed bless you? We have. Our sense of dedication seems greater; our inner peace is not ruled by outward circumstances; His guidance seems clearer, and

---

3   Dallas, TX, Chosen Books/Word Books, 1979

our prayers receive answers. When we set aside a regular time for the Lord, we are more patient, less critical, less angry toward life, more willing to forgive, and more sensitive to others' needs. Even though we have the best of intentions, all too soon, we find ourselves back on the unmanageable merry-go-round of activity and pressure. As we begin to lose our spiritual grip, we need to be "brought up tight" and ask again, "Why did we let this happen?" Thankfully, our own interrogating self-chastisement brings us back to our knees and to our Bibles.

A further confession (See if this is true for you as well as us): our Sunday responsibilities can easily rob us of the worship experience we need even though we are physically sitting right there in the church! We mentally take roll of the choir, "count the house," or worry about some aspect of the order of service. "Will those tenors really hit the high notes on page five?" "Will the sound technician remember to turn on the microphone for the alto soloist before the fourth measure?" Worst of all, an attitude of "I've heard sermons on this text before," dulls our responsiveness. Sometimes our minds race on to some afternoon activity. (How's that for admitting we can be as shallow as the next person?!) But when we set the rudder of our minds to enjoy and to participate in the worship service, committing ourselves to God for that time, sincerely asking that He meet our needs, He does not turn a deaf ear. Somehow He reaches through those layers of distractions running wild in our minds and actually speaks to our hearts.

During our years of marriage, we have had only one Easter Sunday when we were not on a church staff and involved in the planning, preparation, and execution of the services. For that one Easter, instead of working a twenty six hour day, we decided to treat ourselves and our children to a week of "R & R" in Hawaii. As Good Friday and Easter Sunday came closer, we asked ourselves how could we experience worshipping God at this solemn, holy, and celebrative time of year on the warm, white sands of a Maui beach. We had taken a hymnal with us (*Hymns For The Family of God*,[4] of course!) along with our Bibles. (Hotels in Hawaii now have a triple choice: a Gideon Bible, a Book of Mormon, and a Koran.) On Good Friday morning we sat on the beach and designed our own Good Friday service to take place in our room at noon. Just before our service was to begin, the heavens opened, showering the Islands with a driving rain while the four Bocks ran for cover. (We do know enough to come in out of the rain.) We read our Bibles, sang from the hymnal, followed our Order of Worship, and had a wonderful time of praise, meditation, and discussion.

Later that day we saw a poster advertising a hotel-sponsored Easter Sunrise service, and at 6 a.m. on Sunday we made our way to the ballroom where we joined other vacationing worshippers. A small choir and local minister led us. As we started the service, we felt homesick for our own traditions. The room didn't resemble a church in any way, and as the choir sang and the minister began to speak, we both thought to ourselves, "This is truly awful!" The choir sang out of tune and was top-heavy with wobbly female voices. The minister was unimaginative and seemed to lack skill in homiletics. We were accustomed to bright, exciting Easter celebrations

---

4   Grand Rapids, MI, Paragon Associates, Inc. 1976

with good music followed by an excellent sermon. We came to worship, yes, and worship we did, because somehow God tore away our arrogant attitude. He first helped us to recognize our prideful superiority and then let us see that, just like everyone else in the room, we were merely sinners. It was for us that Jesus died and rose again. Yes, in that setting, we were ministered *to*. The hour we spent in the hotel ballroom turned out to be a real highlight of our Hawaiian vacation. It remains in our memory as one of the most meaningful Easters we have ever experienced. The Bock family learned a valuable lesson that year: God is not restricted by physical surroundings or cultural traditions.

At other times we have felt the need to worship out-of-doors. We feel as though we are part of His creation when we can be out there in the midst of His handiwork. Our Bibles and notebooks have traveled to the beach, the mountains, the desert, and to lounge chairs in our own backyard. God seems especially close when we look around and see trees, grass, birds, sky, and flowers. There is something pure and truly therapeutic about the beauty of nature. God's love is beautifully expressed through His creation of nature. Look around you — you'll see His creativity too. What an assurance to know that if we will open the door with receptivity for Him, He will come in to make His presence known.

An old Indian prayer expresses it this way:

> Let me learn the lessons You have hidden in
> every leaf and rock.

Here's an idea of what we look for when we worship in the outdoor cathedrals of this world. It is exciting to view the vast variety of creation. For example, have you ever observed the number of different shades in one color? You will not have to go very far to see the many shades of green in the trees and hedges. Next time you hold a leaf, study the intricacy of its construction. Rocks and flowers, when you look at them closely, are far more involved than you might imagine. Stop . . . and listen to the music of nature: the whispers of the breeze, the melody sung by the birds, the hum of the bees, or the delicate tapping of the rain. This symphony of nature has been orchestrated by the great composer of life. God has given us many unique living creatures to watch and from which to learn. Take a look at the animals and birds in your neighborhood . . . the dogs, cats, squirrels, sparrows, doves, and hummingbirds . . . have you ever observed their different habits? Now think about the people who are close to you: how many different talents and gifts are represented in your small circle of friends? This almost seems like a simplistic exercise for worship, but when you take the time to do it, it puts a whole new meaning into singing songs like, "This Is My Father's World," or "Morning Has Broken." When we become enlightened about God's generosity to His children, we can't help but thank and praise Him. After a time of observation, we look for Scripture passages on nature (the Psalms are full of them) and sing hymns about the beauty of God's creation. Taking the time to thank God for all He has given us makes us receptive to the true spirit of worship and praise.

Another way to avoid spiritual burnout is to associate with people who will give you emotional and spiritual support. We have both learned the value of being a part of a support group or small Bible study, and we highly recommend this. If you are not already involved in such a group, ask God to help you find one to be part of, or better still, start one yourself. It's really not hard, don't feel intimidated. You need not be an educated teacher or theologian because there are many books and tapes available to serve as your guide through any course of study: books like M. Scott Peck's *The Road Less Traveled* [5] or Keith Miller's *Taste of New Wine* [6] are filled with topics for discussion that will appeal and draw out everyone. Select a book from the Bible and do a verse-by-verse study of it. (Bible commentaries will be a big help to you.) You might simply want to get together with caring friends and talk about issues of life. In all cases, it is important that some ground rules be established before beginning any group:

1. Include people who can be trusted. Confidentiality is a must for any kind of sharing group.

2. Everyone must agree on a concept. Will you study a book, a book in the Bible, or just share concerns with each other? And if you study a book or the Bible together, which book will it be?

3. Make sure that everyone feels comfortable praying aloud before any demands are made.

4. The group members need to have compassion for each other. Time together should not be a platform for one member to dominate week after week without allowing others equal time.

---

5   New York, A Touchstone Book, 1978

6   Dallas, TX, Word Books

5. A meeting structure is helpful. Will it go on indefinitely or end at a prearranged time? Which format serves your needs better?

6. Select people who will be consistent participants. Changing the team week after week destroys both continuity and confidentiality. If additional members join, they should only be added with the permission of all. It is sometimes difficult for new folks to join an existing group when they have not shared the same sense of history.

A NOTE FROM FRED: I've always felt that it is not especially wise to be in a group with co-workers. There have been times when the concerns of my heart have to do with working conditions and relationships. I would not feel free to be as open if I were in a group with other staff members. That's why I choose to be in a group of men who are outside my work world. Others may feel differently. I know of one group of music directors here in California who meet at a retreat center a couple of times a year. They find they offer sincere encouragement to each other because they share so many of the same challenges and problems. I know of another group of senior pastors here in Los Angeles who meet once a month to pray and support each other.

We grow in our faith as well as individuals through the loving support system of the Christian community. For several years we have met with Christian friends who not only encourage us, but also hold us accountable for our actions. These friends love us and our family, accept our humanness, listen to our problems, encourage our dreams, and bring us closer to God. Assuming the responsibilities of leadership without these times of give-and-take is impossible for us. If Jesus needed a small group of disciples to surround and help Him in His ministry, what makes us think that we can go it alone? We all need others who will act as a sounding board for our ideas, who will help carry our burdens and who will actually share in our pain. We need people who applaud us when we deserve it, make us feel special, and demonstrate God's love to us. Good friends give us the opportunity to do the same for them. In this kind of close relationship, we are not spiritual leaders, just fellow strugglers in our journey of faith and daily living.

Retreats and conferences can be another source of growth and balance to avoid burnout. Getting away from it all and from the actual working arena often gives a new sense of objectivity as well as spiritual and emotional refreshment. Nowadays, churches realize this, and many offer their own retreat centers. Our church often uses the facilities of Forest Home Christian Conference Center in the Southern California mountains. Times at Forest Home are always refreshing. We look back over the years and see that the giant steps that we and our children have taken on our spiritual walk were done so at Forest Home. Another spiritual filling-station for us has been the annual Praise Gathering for Believers, sponsored by our good friends, Bill and Gloria Gaither, and held each fall in Indianapolis. Inevitably we come home running over with exciting spiritual truths and knowledge, ready to face our world and apply our newly learned lessons. A few days away will relax you and can add mountain-top experiences to valley doldrums that we all have to face during the year.

As far back as either of us can remember and as recently as today, we have been inspired and encouraged by good books. Authors help shape our lives and stimulate growth. We admire and appreciate writers; we do not choose to be spiritual illiterates. We like books of all kinds: clever and wonderful children's literature or background stories shedding light on current events. Our mutual love for books makes for this favorite evening's entertainment: we have dinner early at a favorite restaurant and then go to a nearby bookstore which stays open until 10 p.m. We say goodbye to each other at the front door and then spend the rest of the evening browsing through aisles and aisles of books in our own special interest areas. We meet each other at the cash register a few minutes before closing time. (For the Bocks, this often becomes an expensive evening out!)

Books have been important stepping stones on our spiritual path. Those we have bought have been read and re-read. We asked some of our friends in church ministry to give us a listing of the books that have been the most helpful to them on their spiritual journey. Books can change your life, and any one of these could do so for you. See the BONUS SECTION for this listing.

What does it really mean to live in harmony with God? First, we think that it means to recognize Who He is, and who we are in relationship to Him. Several years ago Fred wrote an anthem called, "Praise His Holy Names." In the lyric, God's many-faceted personality comes into focus by the descriptions of his various names. Just as names such as David, or Gloria, or Michael have special meaning and character, so do God's names. We learn a great deal about God, and who He is, by studying those names and then relating them to His various roles in our lives. Take a look:

Wonderful Counselor
Almighty God
Holy One of Israel
Sun of Righteousness
Chief Cornerstone
Resurrection and the Life
Lamb of God
Son of Man
Lord of all
Lord God Almighty
The Way
The Truth
The Life
Light of the World
Head of the Church
Man of Sorrows
Prince of Peace
Rabbi
Teacher

Master
Shepherd
Savior
Messiah
Redeemer
Advocate
Righteous Judge
Bright and Morning Star
King of kings
Lord of lords
Lord Jesus Christ
Author and Finisher of
    our Faith
Word of Life
God's only Son
I AM
Jesus
Alpha and Omega

He has a name which describes each facet of His character, His many roles, and His ever-changing capacity to meet our pressing needs.

And who are we in relationship to Him? We have different names describing our places in His family:

children	joint heirs
servants	friends
workers	sinners saved by grace
the chosen ones	witnesses
the annointed	

These are a few of the names He uses to describe us. Each of these has a different meaning and characteristic, but the purpose here is to understand how we fit into His plan. In each case He desires to have a relationship and communication with us. When we are out of sync with His plans, our lives reflect pandemonium and discord (perhaps that should be spelled "dis-chord" for our harmonic purposes here.) It is reassuring to realize that the core of our being can be at peace and centered in Him. When that peace is truly experienced, we have indeed found God, for only He can give perfect peace: and having found Him, we have established a relationship with His purposes for His creation. That's what harmony with God is all about!

Chapter II

HARMONY IN THE CHURCH

Part 1 — Harmony with the Congregation

Part 2 — Harmony with the Volunteers

Part 3 — Harmony with the Staff

Part 4— Harmony with the Senior Minister

HARMONY WITH THE CONGREGATION

The church is not a place where the saints gather together, but rather a hospital for the sick: a haven where healing occurs. On any given Sunday in churches all across the country, healing needs to happen and burdens from worry and guilt need to be lifted. As you sit in front of your congregation, can you hear the silent cries of those who are needy, aching, and hungry for spiritual nutrition? For some, the agony is clearly visible and deeply etched on their faces. With others, it is successfully hidden under layers of social graces and the ability to perform as if everything were just fine, thank you.

Next Sunday morning take the time to look around you. Pretend that you are seeing those who have come to worship for the very first time. You will notice some bright, joyful faces eager to participate in praise and worship. These expressions stand out like bright lights in a sea of shadows. And as your eyes move across the rows of worshippers, you might see . . .

> . . . several people aching with an empty loneliness,

> . . . a heartbroken mother who is thinking of a wayward child,

. . . a hurting father who has lost communication with his children,

. . . some who are unemployed and worried about how they will pay this month's bills,

. . . one with head bent low from lack of self-esteem,

. . . one who had to sleep on the streets the previous night,

. . . students disappointed with their academic performances,

. . . children who have been cheated out of love,

. . . those who are physically ill, especially those with a terminal illness,

. . . a young person aimlessly drifting, lacking purpose and goals,

. . . those who have a hardened countenance due to harbored hate and stale resentment,

. . . a married person aching with the failure of a crumbling marriage,

. . . some who are fearfully guarded because they live in a world of constant change and masses of people,

. . . the stooped shoulders of those who carry the unbearable weight of guilt,

. . . a single parent who feels incapable of successfully parenting alone,

. . . those with a vaccuum at the core of their lives
for they have never encountered Jesus
Christ,

. . . some with absolutely no understanding of
God's love and no personal experience of
His forgiving grace,

. . . and many who have never known the joyful,
abundant life of Christ.

They are all part of the colorful human mosaic which
makes up the family of God. As you read this, are you
thinking of folks at your church who fit those descriptions? We are, and if they are sitting in our churches, they
are certainly sitting in the right place! Within the limited
time span of a worship service these people can find
hope and peace. Martin Luther gave us his explanation
for music in this world:

> I wish to see all arts, principally music, in the
> service of Him who gave and created them.
> Music is a fair and glorious gift of God. I
> would not for the world forego my humble
> share of music. Singers are never sorrowful,
> but are merry, and smile through their trou-
> bles in song. Music makes people kinder,
> gentler, more staid and reasonable. I am
> strongly persuaded that after theology there is
> no art than can be placed on a level with
> music; for besides theology, music is the only
> art capable of affording peace and joy of the
> heart . . . the devil flees before the sound of
> music almost as much as before the Word of
> God.

Church music department personnel take notice! This includes directors, organists, soloists and choirs! We have awesome responsibilities: to set a mood by creating an atmosphere where God can speak to His children, to minister to the deepest needs of His people, and to teach through words and music the holiness, greatness, and goodness of our God. Learning to use communication skills is essential in making these things happen. Just as an orator or preacher must utilize communication tools, the basics of the craft and profession, so must we who are involved in church music.

A couple of years ago we went to a play at the Ahmanson Theatre in downtown Los Angeles. We were looking forward to the evening because some well-known, talented actors were starring in this production. The curtain opened to a magnificent stage setting that was full of mysterious atmosphere and which drew applause from the audience when the curtain was first raised. As the scenes unfolded toward intermission, instead of being pleased and caught up in the play, we felt disappointment and anger because it was impossible for us to hear or understand the words of the actors. We sat there for an hour and a half unable to figure out the plot. The audience felt like captive victims. At intermission, we left the theatre, as did many others. We had wasted our evening and our money. When we stopped for coffee at a nearby restaurant, the maitre d' told us his tables filled up most every evening at about intermission time. Lots of folks must have felt the same way we did. The author of that play may have had a wonderful story to tell, but the message did not come across the footlights to the expectantly eager audience. We'll never know what the author wanted us to hear simply because we were robbed of the opportunity to understand what was being said!

As we visit churches, we notice a common problem with most choirs: they don't sing clearly! They bury their heads in their music folders and the words never do get past the printed page of the octavos to reach the eager ears and hearts of those sitting in the pews. At times we've tried to avoid this problem by asking our choir members to look over the congregation, select one specific person, and then as they sing, visualize that they are communicating directly with that one worshipper. In other words, get the message of your music past the footlights.

There needs to be harmony between the importance of enunciation and the quality of the music itself. Comments like, "The music was lovely this morning, but I couldn't understand the words," should make us all feel that we've done only half the job! Certainly, the correct notes were sung, and the sound was lovely, but communication was never established, lives were not changed or inspired.

Another helpful solution to the diction problem is to print the words of the anthem in the church bulletin. Our understanding of the U.S. Copyright Act of 1976 is that this is not a violation, but falls under the "Fair Use" clause of the law. (However, it is very important that all Music Directors understand and abide by the copyright laws, especially regarding the illegal use of photocopied music. PLEASE, PLEASE read the bonus section "The Church Musician and The Copyright Law") Of course, if the anthem is in Latin or French, or German, or Japanese, this really makes good sense. It helps us better communicate our message. Even when the anthem is in English this will be helpful. I jokingly tell my choir that their diction improves 95 per cent when the congregation can read the words while they're being sung!

On the other side of the musical coin is the need for us to use truly excellent music, that has the ability to carry the words deeply into the fibre of our being. There are times when music alone can touch, soothe and heal as nothing else can. Have you ever experienced hearing a symphony, a violin solo or an organ prelude, and been emotionally lifted right out of your seat with the pure beauty of the music itself? Isn't music a wonderful gift from God? And aren't we blessed by Him to be able to use this gift in sharing His love?

FRED: I've been given requests, compliments, and complaints from the best of congregations, including my own. Some worshippers only want to sing the old familiar hymns while others are willing to risk something new. Some would be content if the choir sang only Bach (notice, I didn't say "Bock"), every week. We have some who really prefer listening to simpler gospel songs. I choose to offer a variety, and we have become a musically eclectic church. I make every effort to chose the best of each offering and to request (some might say *demand*) that the choir and soloist prepare and perform their best. We even invite the comments of our worshippers by providing a tear-off sheet in our Sunday morning bulletin. This accomplishes several things: it allows all members of the congregation to register their presence, prayer request, or a message to any staff member. Some weeks I will be given a note that says, "The organ is too loud," followed by another that says, "Please ask the organist to play louder, I can't hear him under the balcony." Obviously, only one of those worshippers can possibly be accommodated. "We can't please all the people all of the time."

What is the level of musical taste of your congregation? Wherever it is, the menu could probably be expanded. I know churches who sing only high-brow "good music," and I also know churches who exist on a musical diet of hymn arrangements and gospel songs sung with accompaniment tracks exactly like the recording artists use. My position on what we sing in church includes both ends of the spectrum. The power to communicate . . . that should be the basis for choosing what we sing. Is the musical selection effective? Does the text say something important? (Does the message of the text complement the message of the minister on Sunday?) Can our choir or soloists present this effectively? Is this selection going to be greeted with groans or appreciation by the choir and by the congregation? Will the congregation be moved by the beauty of the text and music or by our wonderful performance? (Hopefully, you make selection decisions based on better criteria than your congregation's applause! Right?) And then we all have our likes and dislikes to consider as well. Does the choir sing only the music you like?

Spend more time trying to find music that *ministers* and that also has a high level of musical quality as well. The marriage of good lyrics to good music is not terribly easy to come by! Search out the finest.

The human voice is the only instrument that can communicate with both words *and* music. Singers have double power. However, our musical offerings, both the words and the music, need to communicate clearly and to present the very best we can offer. What we're after here are basics of the choral art: clear diction with notes beautifully sung together on the correct pitch. Another basic: keep in mind that music always needs to be the servant of the text. If notes are sung incorrectly, this will certainly destroy clear enunciation. The very best of words or poetry sung to sour notes does not make for a pleasant experience. It is true that the Holy Spirit can and will take what we do, and then bless it and use it to touch hearts. But God deserves our best. Why offer Him anything less? And giving our best requires dedication: an investment of time, more organization, more effort and more preparation. Less than these will result in a mediocre presentation. God honors those dedicated efforts on our part.

"I don't believe in spending too much time on my sermons. I like to allow the Holy Spirit the freedom to speak through me!" stated a minister who was a guest at a friend's dinner party. He honestly thought the Holy Spirit couldn't work through a well-prepared sermon. Comments like that are a weak excuse from one who seemingly does not care to make the necessary commitment and investment of time, energy, or thought. This kind of faulty reasoning sounds more like laziness than spiritual freedom.

Our pastor, Dr. Lloyd John Ogilvie, is just about the most prepared, organized minister we know. During his annual summer study leave, he organizes and outlines his sermons for the coming year. (You'll read more about this in chapter 3.) Here's the amazing part: Lloyd can plan in July to speak on a specific topic some Sunday in January. When that particular Sunday arrives, his message is so timely and pertinent it would appear that he wrote the sermon just hours before to meet our needs for that day. We often limit the Holy Spirit to work within our own time frame. Not so! Our God is the God of yesterday, today and tomorrow. He knows of our needs well in advance, long before we do. The Holy Spirit is capable of working on our behalf before the actual need occurs. And when we are prepared and organized, this makes us a more useable, pliable tool for the Holy Spirit. If lack of preparation is obvious, this will certainly distract and destroy the train of thought. A minister may have a wonderful idea for a sermon: he knows the needs of his church and he knows God's truth can change their lives. But, if his message is buried in a poorly organized outline, with rambling sentences heavily punctuated with "ah, er, a, um," he will not communicate much. We all need to value our congregation enough to be diligent in our homework and preparation. Let's not be like the young student who refuses to study, but at the last minute has the audacity to ask God to help him get an "A" on the exam. (Haven't we all been that young student?) God, as well as teachers, honors preparation. We've also seen many pastors, public speakers and singers who read every word. If there is no eye contact, there is rarely much heart contact. Really good communicators know their material so well that they are not prisoners of the printed page. Secretary of State James Baker was quoted in *Time* with this highly alliterative saying, "Proper preparation prevents poor performance." That's a quote that should be emblazoned on our desks, music stands, choir folders, organs and pianos!

Thank God, performance is certainly not the total story, but it is an important chapter. You and I need to offer our best and then step out of the way allowing God the freedom to do His work in the lives of His children.

Since the subject of this chapter is about creating harmony with our *congregations,* we need to remind ourselves that ultimately, they are our bosses. If they don't like us or what we do, or what we stand for, we can start packing our bags. As in any relationship, an acceptable friendship between choir director and congregation is an on-going, growing relationship built on trust. If you lead your congregation to new expressions, and they trust you, and you in return don't let them down, hurt them, embarrass them or insult them, they will probably let you do it again. A helpful caution sign reads, "Take it slow, my friend, and take it easy!" "Rome was not built in a day" was never truer than in this relationship. Along the way we need to be sensitive to the traditions of the congregation and church we serve. Often we hear stories about ministers of music who are newly hired and march into the job like a bull going into a china shop. They are so anxious to make the program their own, that they throw out all that is precious and cherished about the existing program. That does nothing but create a lack of trust and misunderstanding. We do need to hear the congregation's comments and suggestions (and implement some of the better ones, and give them credit, too!), and we need to remember and respect what their church music heritage is built upon. Let the church know that you plan to preserve what is useful, meaningful, and beautiful about the programs of your predecessors and the traditions of the church.

One way to let the parishioners know that you value their opinions and taste is to do a choir presentation of favorite anthems. Let the congregation or members of the choir suggest what to sing, and then do it. This could easily become an annual event, and my guess is that a concert like this would win a lot of grass-roots support for your musical program, as well as for you as a person.

Another word of caution in dealing with the congregation: do not think of yourself more highly than you ought. While it is true that you are the Minister of Music, you're still a person just as they are. And while you and I agree that in that role, you probably are the most informed and knowledgeable person on the staff or in the congregation when it comes to church music, don't advertise this on your sleeve. Don't let everyone know how smart you are. (This kind of advice works whether you are a Minister of Music, a teacher, or a milkman.) When it comes to music, everyone has his likes and dislikes, but likes do differ from person to person. It is your job to try to please both.

And lastly, be part of the congregation yourself. Don't hold yourself aloof or separate from the congregation. Be available, be friendly, and on a first name basis with as many church members as you can. Go to congregational meetings; be a part of the men's or women's Fellowship group; participate or join a small group or Bible study; do some home visitation, hospital calling, whatever you can to get to know the people of your church. Then you're not just the hired choir director who shows up for rehearsal and Sunday services; you're part of the Family! After all, keeping harmony with the congregation is very much like keeping harmony within your own family.

Part 2

HARMONY WITH THE VOLUNTEERS

A worship service that meets the needs of people takes the co-operation and teamwork of many. It is not just the responsibility of the minister and the music department. It also involves the lay persons of the congregation who volunteer their time, energy and talent to create an atmosphere of reverence. If they do their jobs well, we are almost unaware of their presence. But if they don't, we all are made blantantly aware of them. For example, the people who operate the sound equipment and the light controls. If a soloist can pick up a microphone and have it on and ready to go, it adds to the smooth flow of the service. If not, it causes embarrassment not only for the soloist, but also for the sound person, as well as some annoyance for the worshippers who can't hear. Sometimes a few measures of music are sung in silence only to be followed by a blaring of the soloist's voice when the equipment is finally turned on. The same is true of the light technician. When we stand to sing a hymn or read the responsive reading, it is much easier if we can see the printing on the page!

Directors of Music are certainly not in charge of every aspect of a service, but input from him or her can be helpful to the cohesiveness of the service. Potential problems can be solved in advance if both these volunteers are given copies of the bulletin and then told *when* to turn up the lights or sound. Color-coded markers do wonders for drawing attention to a possible trouble spot in the service. If the sound cues can be marked with a yellow highlighter and the lighting cues in pink, it should be obvious *before the time* when his or her attention is needed. That may sound simplistic, in fact so simplistic that no one has ever suggested it. Maybe the dedicated people who serve God by turning on the lights or microphones during a service have never had anyone explain the concept of planning ahead to achieve the benefits of a smooth-running service. If these volunteers understand how important they are to the tone and flow of worship, they will pobably make an effort to stay one step ahead in the order of the service.

Ushering is another area of importance to the flow of worship. This is a vital link between the outside world and the spirit of worship within the sanctuary walls.

LOIS: We have a long-standing tradition at Hollywood Presbyterian Church of having a team of well-trained ushers. On almost any given Sunday, our head-usher can feel proud of the job his ushers do. Recently, however, the plan fell apart in the balcony because of the lack of thought on the part of one usher. Let me tell you how I, as a needy worshipper, felt that morning. I had had a hectic week with a great deal of stress and disappointments. I desperately needed to experience God and His touch of peace. I went into the sanctuary earlier than usual so that I could sit and meditate quietly. Slowly others began to fill the

48

church. The pew I occupied was almost full, when an unthinking and untrained usher motioned to two late-comers to join us. The only two available seats were on the opposite aisle, and the newcomers had to step on the feet of every person they passed. Just as the choir stood to sing its first anthem, a baby with healthy lungs, unwisely positioned with his parents in the front row of the balcony, started screaming in a key that differed from the choir! When it came time for the offering, a collection plate was started from the right aisle. Suddenly, the same unaware usher started one from the left aisle. They both reached me in the middle simultaneously. There I sat with two offering plates! By the time the minister began his sermon, my mind was so diverted that I found it difficult to focus on his message. The experience of worship was wasted on me. The lack of skill and thinking on the part of that one usher had distracted a good number of people in the balcony.

That kind of story does not happen too often. But it does happen occasionally and such scenes are repeated in churches across the country each Sunday. Can you relate to that experience? Let's think about how we can avoid disasters and include our ushers in the process of worship.

Ushers are an extremely important part of our worship service and church. They are like the Old Testament Doorkeepers. Psalm 84:10 says,

I would rather be a doorman of the Temple of
my God than live in palaces of wickedness.
(The Living Bible)

A doorman is one who extends a hand of welcome. He or she, (yes, we do have women ushers and greeters), is the representitive for the staff, the church, and the Lord Himself. We live in a world of harrassed people, living with and bearing tremendously stressful burdens. We get used to seeing scowls on brows and hearing voices of disdain, indifference, and anger. It is such a pleasant experience to walk up the stairs to the narthex of our church and be met by an usher who greets everyone with a smile on his face and an outstretched hand of welcome.

Why do people come to church anyway? Some come from habit, of course, but even those who are there habitually must receive some renewal, revitalization, or respite from their frantic or boring lives. Knowing that this hour of worship is crucial to their spiritual and emotional lives makes it important that everything possible be done to make the worship service fulfill the personal needs of those who have taken their time to fill our pews.

An usher is sometimes the only person who speaks to a visitor, especially in a large, more impersonal church. Ministers and choirs speak to the masses, but the individual attention of an usher is imperative in setting a tone of warmth and care. Everyone, regardless of position or status in life, needs and wants to feel loved and cared for.

Ushers at our church are given three responsibilities:

1. Greeting,
2. Seating,

3. Collecting the offering.

The greeting is important to the individual, and the seating is important to the service. We do not seat people during a prayer or a musical selection. We indicate by asterisk ** in the bulletin when people may to be guided to their pews. (See sample bulletins on pages 197-208.) This avoids unnecessary interruptions, which break the spirit of the service.

Our ushers urge parents to take babies to the church nursery. Some new mothers and fathers prefer to hold their infants during the service. If that happens, every effort is made to seat them near the back of the church (if those seats aren't already taken by those arriving at church early!)

Happiness is

getting to church early enough to get a back seat.

How disconcerting for an entire congregation to listen to a baby crying in competition with the minister's sermon or the sacred music. We love babies (we've had two of our own), but they are better off in a crib out of earshot of the worshippers. This can be a touchy matter with some parents who are totally unaware that the actions and noises of their precious child can be an intrusion in the service!

The third responsibility of ushers is taking the offering. This can be done in a planned, rehearsed order. If the head usher will take time to train these people to walk down the aisle in pairs, to assign rows, confusion disappears.

It is also helpful if ushers wear a carnation or a name badge which is identifiable. We have been in churches where the ushers wear morning coats with striped trousers. In our church, all ushers wear dark suits with carnations in their lapels. If there are guidelines for apparel, you can avoid the chance that some extrovert usher will parade down the aisle attired in plaid slacks and a bright red blazer, looking ready for a Caribbean cruise.

Let us suggest that you (or the church administrators) prepare a MANUAL FOR USHERS. If this handbook is available for all who volunteer for this important responsibility, it will make their job easier and your service flow smoother. It is important that ushering be taken seriously and handled as carefully as any other responsiblity in the church. This is also a ministry within the body of the Christian Church, requiring the gifts of loving and caring, a dedicated sense of commitment, and a desire to do everything right and in good order.

As we work with our church volunteers and staff, let's keep our goals *before us and them* as a unified body of believers desiring to worship and please God! Let's do all we can to remove barriers of distrust, lack of communication, and the tendency to put the musicians of the church center stage. Because we are a performing arm of the church, we are certainly more likely to receive applause, praise, and recognition. In reality, however, the musicians are no more deserving than the Sunday School teachers, ushers, or the church treasurer. Only as we work together, dream together, pray together, and support each other will we experience true harmony in our church.

It often is easy for the Music Department members to appear to be a clique or an exclusive club. One way to live in harmony with your congregation is to break down those obstacles that separate the musically gifted from those whose gifts lie in other areas. Let us suggest some ways this can be done. Music staff and choir members:

1. Join Bible studies or Sunday School classes with other parishioners.

2. Volunteer to teach a Vacation Bible School class.

3. Be singing waiters or waitresses at a church dinner. And if you are really serious about being "one of the gang," offer to help with the dishes!

4. Serve on church committees, Session or Deacon Boards.

5. Raise money for a church project. (See Harmony in the Choir chapter for more details on this.)

Members of our choirs have done all of the above, and we have found that it increases our credibility as leaders of worship in the Sunday morning service.

I Corinthians 14:12 says:

> So it is with you, since you are eager to have
> spiritual gifts, try to excel in gifts that build up
> the church.

A rich and rewarding experience results when our spiritual gifts and musical talents are used, and lives are changed, commitments deepened, sins forgiven, and broken spirits healed. Let's continually remind ourselves that there would be no need to form a choir, spend hours rehearsing and perfecting our skills, if we had no congregation to join us and share in the uplifting, joyful experience of worshipping God through our music.

Part 3

HARMONY WITH THE STAFF
(Fred's thoughts on hiring
Music Department Staff)

Hiring an organist is not an easy job. I suppose the job is easier if you have someone in mind—one who is very talented and whom you have wanted to secure for a long time and who suddenly has become available just at the same time you have an open spot. You simply "go get 'em!" That sounds rather quixotic, doesn't it? Back to the real world! In the course of twenty years or so, I've had to hire five or six organists and in two cases have had to request resignations. Each procedure requires some extensive homework, knowledge and an abundance of prayer.

If you are in a position where you can audition several people for the job, you will have a choice, and hopefully you will be able to secure the services of the best one for your church. I mention this, because often there is no choice. When the Smith family gives the new organ to the church, it often comes with strings attached — namely that Milly Smith (of course!) be the church organist. Or, Milly Smith, age 94, has been the church organist for 57 years! (She was hired back in 1933 and told that the job was hers as long as she wanted it.) Often the pastor's wife is the spouse-appointed organist; another potential trouble spot for sure. These are tough, no-win situations and I don't envy anyone who finds himself stuck in this predicament. Lest you get the wrong idea, there are pastor's wives who are superb organists and I've heard of a few 90 year old organists who still have it! But, for argument's sake, let's say you are in a position to scout around and find just the right organist for your church.

Now how to go about that . . . other directors would be my first source to tap. Call a few colleagues and see if they have any recommendations. When you call, be prepared to tell the details of the position: how many services, (Sunday morning and evening, plus a mid-week?), rehearsal schedules, kind of instrument, quality of instrument, church membership requirement, salary, vacation, insurance, weddings, funerals, (Is there extra payment for these? And is the organist required to attend the wedding *rehearsals?*) Cover all the basics of the job. Is the salary and compensation offered commensurate with other churches of your size? Are you in the same ballpark? When you start making some calls, contact folks who have programs and musical tastes similar to yours. Calling a Christian Science Church will bring you a different kind of organist than you'd find at an Assemblies of God, or Full Gospel church.

As you begin your search, you'll find that organists have questions of their own to ask. They will certainly want to know if the organ is a pipe organ or an electronic one. If you have an antiquated, inferior instrument, you'll not have a line of unemployed organists waiting to apply. Another query they want to make is about the reverberation quality of the sanctuary. Is the room "dead" or "alive"? Is the sound one that echoes when the organist stops playing or is it swallowed up like it would be in a heavily carpeted, sound-absorbant living room? And organists who are highly qualified and do some organ teaching on the side will want to know if the church organ is avilable for them to use for lessons.

We would want to make certain that any organist hired is a committed believer in Jesus Christ. It also helps if they have a strong church background. And it's terrific if their church background is similar to your church's tradition. Personally I prefer organists who have grown up with a strongly evangelical background and then have gone on to study organ seriously in a major university setting; they get the best of both worlds. Ideally we want someone who can really play the organ well, knows all the standard organ repertoire, can read and play all the notes, can fill in the holes with some creative improvisation, lead the congregation in their singing of hymns, and be able to play *Jesus Loves Me,* or *Alleluia* without the printed music should the minister, all-of-a-sudden, decide to sing those songs. Organists who can do all that are difficult to find! But once you have found one, as the song says, "Never let her (or him) go."

Okay, now you have a listing of organists who come highly recommended to you by various friends who are also in a similar church situation. You might wish to form a search committee to hear the auditions of the organists, or perhaps to help locate other applicants. If you get 300 applications, you'll need to devise some list of qualifying questions to narrow it down to the finalists. In most cases, to be honest, there were only four or five qualified candidates. (This is because I was quite emphatic about what I was looking for, and was truthful and thorough about the job requirements, enabling both the applicant and myself to discern early-on who was and who was not a prospect.) To make life easier and to avoid having to come to the church seven times to hear one organist each time, why not schedule an evening or two? And if you enlist a small committee they can help you in the decision. (Unless you'd rather do it alone and not get into "committee" politics.) Be fair and allow each organist some time to try out the instrument on his or her own, in private, prior to the audition.

As to the content of the audition itself, I differ from many of my colleagues. It is my personal feeling that the major purpose of the organist's position in a church is to support, lead and bring excitement to the congregational singing. The next purpose is to provide organ music that supports the worship service. These aspects of the job are, to my way of thinking, more important than the playing of virtuoso organ pieces. While there's certainly nothing wrong with using the great organ repertoire of the masters, this is not the major emphasis. So, if the would-be organist is looking for a position to show off his or her "stuff," I'm not so sure our church is the place for them!

To make the applicant feel comfortable and at ease, I ask them to play, full organ, a stately hymn such as *Holy, Holy, Holy*. Then I ask them to play it again, and when they get to the end, *ad lib* 4-8 bars in a stately style that builds into full organ with reeds, or perhaps sforzando on. Modulate up a half-step higher, and then play the hymn again, this time with some interesting harmonies . . . *not* the hymnbook variety . . . ending with a big, full,

"Amen." If they do not do this well, if the interlude sounds like a Beginning Theory I assignment, then I can tell right then and there that this is not the organist for me! Next on my "must be able to do" list is to play something soft and pretty for about 20 seconds in the key of Ab, modulating to the key of E major. This will really put them to the test because many organists cannot modulate or improvise their way out of a paper bag. If 20 seconds stretches into two minutes and they are still hopelessly floundering in Ab, call it quits right there. The ability to modulate and improvise is a strong requirement for my organist to be sure. He/she must play as ushers seat worshippers and while babies are being baptized or dedicated, must "kill time" while the offering is received, or fill that lull just before the wedding march begins. There are lots of places where improvisation is a definite necessity. If the applicant has survived the ordeal thus far, ask him or her to play *Jesus Loves Me.* No book, no page number, just right off the top of their heads — play it. If they play it in the key of F, you're in trouble. (High F's at 9:30 in the morning don't make it at all!) Eb is adequate, but C is better.

Next, I feel that accompanying the choir and soloists are two strong organist responsibilities. I ask the organist to follow my directing of a well-known hymn, like *A Mighty Fortress Is Our God,* which has holds and stops and starts in it. Next I ask the applicant to follow my directing in an anthem that is being sight-read. (As with potential choir members' auditions, I bring with me an easy, medium, and difficult anthem for sight-reading purposes.)

When all this has been done and we are rather pleased with the results (bear in mind that organists get nervous under such trying circumstances, just like we do!) then, and only then, do I ask to hear the repertoire they have prepared for us to hear. It will usually be a commanding piece of organ music that shows off both the organ and the organist. Audition pieces should always include a Bach *Prelude and Fugue,* and other representative music from the various eras: Baroque, Classical, Romantic, and Contemporary. You'll want to hear at least part of the pieces in these categories. I think by the time you get to this point, you'll know whether or not this is a potential organist for your church.

Let me repeat that in fairness to the organist and your committee, it is best to spell out exactly what you are looking for either on the phone or in a letter, before the lengthy procedure of an audition. It will save you time and it is the polite thing to do for applicants.

To then decide which of the applicants . . . their musical skills being equal, . . . you will hire, now depends on other more subjective criteria. Are your personalities compatible? Is this position one that the organist's family will be enthusiastic about (or is the organist moving from a church where his or her family attends and they all will be uprooted by the change?) Does he or she have a history of changing jobs every year or two? Is the salary agreeable? Go with your hunches here. If you feel better toward one applicant than the another, respond to those feelings. Ask the Lord to guide you and direct you in this crucial selection process.

Equal care and concern should be exercised in hiring anyone who serves in the Music Department of the church: additional directors for other choirs, soloists, handbell directors, pianists, and a Music Department secretary. Many of the same qualifications we looked for in the hiring of a church organist are qualities we look for in other employees: their general musical knowledge, their style of playing or directing, their personal faith, and their ability to get along with others. As with all staff members, it is important that each know to whom he or she is responsible. Problems can occur when the chain of command is not clearly understood.

A director for children's choirs certainly needs be an enthusiastic, energetic and joyful communicator with young singers. Soloists need not only sing beautifully, but should have a comprehensive repertoire, as well as a thorough knowledge of vocal production problems and solutions. Pianists should be expected to read music exceptionally well, be ready to assist and support the Directors in choir rehearsals by playing voice parts as well as accompaniments. In searching for a handbell director, you will want to find someone who has extensive knowledge of handbell techniques and literature from beginning to advanced ringers. And in selecting a Music Department secretary, keep in mind that one is needed who: works well with volunteers, can keep schedules, manages the office efficiently, and makes a good impression for you and for the entire department when dealing with people in person or on the phone. (This person will often be your spokesperson.)

When you have selected your group of assistants, it is important to let them know how they are doing in their work. I would honestly have to admit that sometimes I get so involved in my own world that I forget to stop and communicate my feelings of appreciation. I know it is important so I am trying to be aware of my colleagues' contributions. Meet with them often, review upcoming plans, share with them your insights and overall departmental plans. Encourage them to broaden their own perspectives in their special fields by taking additional courses, attending workshops and seminars to implement their skills and production. Then you can dream and pray together as a staff. There needs to be a good, solid foundation of harmony built *within* the Music Staff as well as with the entire church staff.

FIRING

Let's hope that everyone you hire turns out to be everything you ever expected and stays with you on the most pleasant of terms for years and years. Having to fire someone from a church position is never easy, and I don't recommend it unless there is absolutely no other alternative. Even for churches, and other non-profit organizations, there are laws today regarding hiring and firing practices. You'll need to check with a local attorney who handles employee-employer relations to get further information, as ordinances and rulings vary from city to city and state to state. If you find no other option, then you'd better have a very strong case for dismissal with plenty of documentation, citing the problems which have been shared with the employee, in the presence of a witness, over a period of time. There should be a letter following each confrontation reiterating the grievances discussed with a specific due-date when change must happen, or else dismissal will occur. A meeting like this should happen more than once, and over a period of time, say three months to one year. If dismissal is the only solution, I strongly suggest the church secure counsel before proceeding with a firing.

Dismissal of a staff member is certainly a sad duty. However, this must sometimes occur in order to keep harmony within the staff.

Part 4

HARMONY WITH THE SENIOR MINISTER

It was lunch time. We were attending a choral workshop along with a few hundred others. Our voices were tired from the plethora of music we had sung for the past three hours. We were slow to arrive in the hotel ballroom. We found a table with two empty spots, introduced ourselves to the eight people who were already eating their salads (drowned in too much bleu-cheese dressing).

We entered a conversation already in progress in which an animated gentleman related his woes. He felt that his once-successful music program was being undermined by a new minister with very definite musical opinions, which didn't match his or those of the choir. This, coupled with the new minister's enormous ego, had reduced a choir of fifty members to one of about twenty. The minister accomplished all this destruction in only one short year.

After this conferee had shared his story of discouragement, a woman across the table openly told us how her minister had created low spirits in the music department by treating the musicians and singers with indifference and lack of support. Together, as we chased the over-baked chicken breasts around our plates, we empathized with her as she said, "I think I'll just have to get out of the church music business. It's too difficult to get along with ministers." That does seem to be the most common complaint of choir directors.

But wait, there is another script to be read, one written by pastors. The theme is basically the same, but the "bad guy" character is now the music director. The cries of many ministers are "How can I ever get along with the musicians on my staff?" One minister said, "Our choir director is so stubborn, he refuses to teach the choir anything that was written after the 18th century. I'm so tired of anthems being sung in Latin." "I know the position is just part-time, but why can't our director be better organized? She is late and doesn't know how to run a rehearsal, so the choir members get discouraged. How can we expect the choir to give its best, when the director doesn't?" And one lament we've heard often is "Why is it that musicians are so moody?"

Why are complaints so plentiful from both pastors and ministers of music? Have you heard any of these comments uttered from your own mouth? Or have any such comments been made about you? If so, read on with an open mind and a pure heart. We believe that we as members of the church staff should serve as models of what it means to love one another. How can we implore society to live at peace if we as Christians can't work together?

Maybe we should start with a basic principle:

Never is the need for team spirit greater
than it is on a church staff!

What is a team? The minister, the director of music, and the entire church staff! Does that sound like a simple enough beginning? A clear understanding is truly fundamental to the success of your relationship. A team is two or more persons working together with the *same goal* in mind.

Let's take a few minutes for some honest soul-searching. If you can better clarify your thoughts by writing them down, pick up your pencil.

1. What are the goals that you and your minister share?

2. What do you like and admire about your pastor?

3. What do you think your pastor should like and admire about you?

4. What is the obstacle in your relationship that prohibits reaching your common goals?

5. What constructive, positive action can *you* take that will help build a good working team spirit with your pastor?

Our church has a senior pastor and several associate ministers. I can honestly say that we all share the same goal. Our methods for reaching that goal might differ, but we all desire to work together unifying the worship service, so that everything focuses on the central theme, the Lord Jesus Christ. The worship service then becomes more than a presentation; it becomes communication and preparation for the people of God to meet Him and face their world.

If personality conflicts cloud your focus, something needs to be done to dissipate those clouds.

A foundation of clear understanding must be laid about this most crucial issue: *Who Is The Boss?* Were this the business world, the senior pastor would fill the role of President of the Corporation or Chairman of the Board. That makes him the boss! And the choir director? Well, he or she is the Vice President in charge of music. With that line of authority understood, life should be easier for both of you. You may have an agenda you wish to implement, but if the minister disagrees, you will probably have to submit to his wishes. We know that's a bitter pill to swallow sometimes, but someone has to be in charge. We've never known a corporation to operate efficiently with all chiefs and no Indians.

For others, however, this may not be a problem at all, because you enjoy a good working relationship. Let's consider some ways to build a better team. Essential to any good relationship is the amount of time you spend together. Make an effort to become friends with open communication about both negative and positive feelings. If your minister hasn't initiated a time to work either on the worship service or on your personal relationship with him, then you be the one to make the first move. Approach him honestly, in a non-threatening way, sharing your desire to have a friendship and to work out the problems. He'll probably not turn you down.

By establishing a consistent appointment with each other you can begin to think together, pray together, dream together and hope together so that the music and the sermons equip your congregation for their ministry in the world. Develop a mutual respect for each other's talents and gifts. Let's face it, you and I can't preach sermons, and our ministers probably would not know how to teach a choir of volunteers to sing like angels.

Lloyd and I meet on Thursday afternoons, sometimes just the two of us, and sometimes we include our worship team to review the upcoming Sunday services. We recognize that each person has his or her own responsibilties and talents, and as we meet together weekly, we have grown to appreciate each other. Each person contributes to the success of our church service, from the prelude and call to worship to the benediction and postlude. That includes the administrative tasks that must be done before the doors are opened on Sunday morning: ordering flowers for the chancel, preparing the bulletin, training the team of ushers, maintaining the church facility, preparing the lessons for the Sunday School classes, and managing the thousand and one secretarial chores. Each is equally important. We must learn to value and mutually respect every member of the church body. Each contributes to the whole of the worship experience.

It is reassuring to know that the pastor values the musical presentation as something more than just a preliminary to the *real* worship, his sermon. He recognizes music as an actual part of the worship experience in and of itself. One Sunday after a particularly moving anthem, our pastor stood and said to the hushed congregation, "I feel that I have just been ministered to by the choir. That's one of the best sermons I've ever heard." Every member of the choir felt especially appreciated that morning.

Lloyd and I have established a friendship apart from the professional side of our relationship. It does help if you are on the same cultural as well as the same spiritual wave-length.

We find it rewarding to be friends as individuals. This friendship includes our families. Our children all like each other, which pleases us. We can go out to dinner or to a play and honestly enjoy each other's company. That definitely benefits our working relationship.

We recognize that we are both creative persons and that we should be catalysts for each other. Often we receive some note of appreciation or kind thought from Lloyd or one of his associates. Nothing brightens our day more than opening the mail and finding such a note.

Why is it so difficult to express appreciation to someone who works for and with us? Could it be our own insecurities? We have heard of some ministers who are so protective of their own turf that they can never express kindness or appreciation to their music staff or to the choirs. For them a reprimand or criticism is easier than a simple "thank you." This is also true of some choir directors, who find it difficult to stand before their choir and say, "Thank you! You are terrific!" If you find that so, examine the reasons why. We urge you to allow yourself freedom in expressing and feeling appreciation. Life will become more pleasant!

In a good relationship there is also the element of encouraging personal growth. This takes listening to each other, laughing together, and growing together. We have learned that to place another person on a pedestal is unfair. We cannot and should not expect perfection from another living person, because it is impossible to live up to those kinds of lofty expectations. Where can he or she go but down? We need to give each other the freedom to make mistakes and to be fallible.

If we are secure in our friendship and our motives are above question, then when we are disappointed in the actions of each other, we have earned the right to be heard. In a loving, caring way we can hold each other accountable for our actions.

A basic church principle: WE NEED EACH OTHER!

Pastoring in a church is not easy! Burnout is very high in this profession. Sometimes when we hear Christians criticizing their pastor or members of the church staff, we want to question them: Why don't you spend the same amount of time supporting and praying for your minister as you do critizing? Armchair quarterbacking is easy. Try walking in his shoes, keeping his schedule, carrying the burdens of the counseling hours and see how you would fare. Moreover, church members often give nice gifts to their pastors with "strings attached." They want special favors or expect the minister to include them in the decision-making process of the church. This makes some pastors suspicious about accepting gifts.

We believe that the best ways to support our minister are to be his friend, to pray for him, to be available to him when he wants to talk, to keep his conversations confidential, and to show him our appreciation. Like the rest of the world, he wants to be recognized, valued, and respected. Stop the idle gossip. Negative feelings and comments will not help to create a better relationship or reach mutual goals.

Retain as open a mind as you possibly can. It is human nature to be defensive when someone criticizes. However, if we can ask God to help us sift through the grains of seemingly harsh words, we may learn valuable lessons and become deeper, more caring men and women. Not everything we do, or everything that our pastoral staff does is perfect. We do make mistakes from time to time and need to learn lessons from our failures as well as from our successes.

Conflicts are created at times, not because someone is wrong, but because we have different tastes. Some people choose to worship in a very austere, majestic setting, while others want a warm, tender, relational setting. Ideally, both sides should be interwoven into the tapestry of worship, but if this is not possible, someone has to give in to the other's cultural taste.

If you feel you *cannot* work out your differences, we have a hard-line suggestion. Get out! Neither of you will reach your potential if you are running in opposite directions. You are both suffocating the spiritual growth of your congregation with bad attitudes, lack of excitement for the work, and depleted support of the ministry. In addition, working in such constant conflict will not encourage you to expand your musical abilities to develop your creativity, or to stimulate you to a deeper walk with God. Move on to new, fertile soil, where you can find a pastor you respect and like.

Remind yourself of the ultimate purpose: to sing and to speak with eternal values in mind. The goal is to lead people to a relationship with Jesus Christ.

Chapter III

HARMONY WITH THE CHOIR

Part 1 — Turning a Choir Into a Family

Part 2 — The Outreach of the Choir

Part 3 — What to Do Prior to the Choir Season

Part 4 — What to Do Prior to Every Rehearsal

Part 5 — Running a Smooth Rehearsal

Part 6 — What to Do Before the Next Rehearsal

Part 7 — "The Best Laid Plans . . . "

Part 1

TURNING A CHOIR INTO A FAMILY

Harmony in the choir is absolutely crucial! The most obvious harmony is music itself. No one wants to hear a choir that does not harmonize and sing in tune. To some, a choir singing flat or sharp is as painful as a dentist's drill. But there is another kind of harmony and it too is crucial: the harmony that establishe ; unity and love within the choir family. For some of you that means creating a bonding relationship with ten to fifteen people, and for others it will mean blending with over a hundred. (Did you know the average church choir is under twenty people?) We address these words to all of you, whether you're creating heavenly sounds with a dozen voices or 120. Whatever the size of your choir, the task of producing harmony is not an easy one.

The music program at our church is a large one, because of the size of our church. First Presbyterian Church of Hollywood has over 4200 members plus hundreds of regular visitors. We are fortunate in that we can draw from a large number of talented people within our congregation, but that certainly doesn't mean our music program is more *successful* or better than anyone else's. (Fred does admit, however, that serving in a church with a good-sized choir makes being a choir director more *fun!*) We are also quick to tell you that when you head a large church music program, the headaches occur more often and are bigger! More people means the potential for more complaints and more problems. More hands to hold, yes, but the plus side means more members to be helpful to, supportive of, and involved in the music ministry.

FRED: I often refer to the Cathedral Choir at the First Presbyterian Church as a wonderful instrument to play. I feel grateful to have inherited this group and the entire music program of our church. We are part of a long rich history which began in 1941, when Dr. and Mrs. Charles Hirt were asked to develop a graded choir program. They were so successful in their endeavors that churches across the country copied their organizational ideas, style and plans. Charles and Lucy remained as the beloved and respected leaders of this church music program for thirty years. Their creative ideas were worthy of becoming our traditions. As architects and administrators, they built and established a program that demanded and received:

> Commitment to Christ,
>
> Commitment to His Church,
>
> Commitment to the choir,
>
> Commitment to each other.

The bylaws of the Cathedral Choir were written during those early formative days. They've been updated, revised, and are still in use today. Each of our choir members is given a Membership Directory at the beginning of the choir year, and the bylaws are included in the back of this little booklet for handy reference. That way the officers know exactly what their responsibilities are. The bylaws are very thorough, and they work extremely well! If you want to organize or re-organize your choir program, these bylaws clearly spell out responsibilities and duties. You'll probably find some points here that might be useful in delegating responsibilities in your music program. The Cathedral Choir of the First Presbyterian Church of Hollywood has given us permission to share these with you. They can be found in the back of this book under the RESOURCE MATERIALS.

Over the years, we have found that people are pretty much the same no matter where they live or what church they attend. People in your choirs are probably very similar to those in ours. Choirs do seem to be a microcosm of the greater church or even of our society in general. Whatever problems and joys can be found *outside* the rehearsal room or choir loft, you can find right *within* your own choir:

Saintly people sitting beside lukewarm Christians;

Wealthy people and some on the verge of bankruptcy;

Singles who wish they were married, and marrieds who wish they were single;

Parents who can hardly wait for their children to grow up and leave home, and expectant couples who eagerly await the birth of their first child;

Intellectuals who thrive on learning new truths conversing with those who haven't read a book in years;

Energetic members holding down three jobs harmonizing with some who can't seem to hold on to one;

Outgoing personalities befriending those who are insecure and shy;

Givers giving and takers taking — a seemingly natural behavior for each.

They all meet together on common ground, their enjoyment of singing, their need to be loved and belong to the Christian family, and their desire to be part of a ministry that leads others in worship through music. Their motives are in sync and sung in harmony!

In many ways the director of music is a minister to the members of the music department and to the choirs: a spiritual leader as well as a music leader, a shepherd of the flock. One friend of ours is appropriately called the "Music Pastor".

FRED: I accepted the offer to become the Director of Music at our church during the first part of July, 1981, I was apprehensive and nervous, but I was also very excited. My days were already full to the brim, and frankly, I wasn't looking for something else to do. After lots of conversation with Lois and soul searching on my part, I decided to give it a try. My first time with the choir was at their annual retreat over Labor Day weekend. Lois said, "We can't go into that group feeling like we don't know them. We must spend some time in prayer for them." We requested a list of the choir members, and each day we prayed for a specific person and worked at memorizing names. When we arrived at the retreat that Friday afternoon, we already felt spiritually bonded to each individual choir member. That weekend we were able to put faces with names that were imprinted in our minds. We continue today to pray for these dear friends and their families.

We soon discovered that the biggest cohesive element in the Cathedral Choir is that of prayer. Time after time we have witnessed God's care and concern for His children in our choir. One of the blessings of membership in the Cathedral Choir is the comfort and assurance that each one feels knowing that choir friends pray for guidance, healing, and forgiveness. Repeatedly we have rejoiced as jobs have been found, family members healed, marriages mended, and spiritual growth encouraged.

The Cathedral Choir, perhaps like the choir at your church, is a unique blend of very different and gifted personalities who possess a genuine affection for one another. They demonstrate repeatedly, in many tangible ways, just how much they care about one another. They spend time together, they fix and deliver dinners to each other's homes during an illness, they loan money, and in many cases have made outright monetary gifts to a member in financial need. They are truly good friends. They are a family!

Part 2

THE OUTREACH OF THE CHOIR

These choir members also have concern for the world outside the walls of the rehearsal room. Each Christmas, the Executive Committee selects a needy family in our church to be the recipient of the choir's Christmas gift. Money is donated and gifts are purchased for the selected folks. We are able to give a happy Christmas where there would have been none.

There have also been on-going mission projects for the last few years. Each Thursday night a red velvet bag is passed around during rehearsal and as a result of the choir's generosity:

— plane tickets have been purchased for missionaries to travel to and from their fields,

— an earthquake-damaged church has been repaired,

— a sound system has been purchased for a youth coffee house in Hollywood,

— contributions have been given to an agency which cares for abused children,

— regular monthly support is raised for a missionary from our own church whose parents and brother are in the Cathedral Choir,

— gifts have been given to a classroom of under-privleged children, taught by the daughter of a choir member,

— airfare was given to help a disabled person receive medical treatment at a hospital in Pennsylvania.

The first year alone, over $6000 in loose change was collected in that little red bag. And this is *above and beyond* their regular giving to our church budget. This kind of caring and giving does wonders, not only for the surprised recipients, but also for the unification of the choir as well. We notice that this giving spirit pervades all of the choirs in our church. Last Christmas many needy children received brightly wrapped, brand new toys from the big-hearted members of the Festival Choir (another adult choir in our church). And from the looks of our music library, which served as their storage area, there must have been many smiling faces on Christmas morning. Repeatedly we hear reports about groups or individuals in our Music Department who have demonstrated an act of Christian love and kindness. We know that as members of this family, we must not only be concerned for each other, but that we must also *do* something. Magnanimous feelings and thoughts without positive actions are dead.

Another successful outreach has been the annual Variety Show put on by the Cathedral Choir. By design, it is *not* religious in content. The program consists of Broadway show tunes, songs from great movie musicals, tap dancing, and brief comedy skits. This show is not performed in the sanctuary, but in our Fellowship Hall which is far more suited to this type of presentation. All choir members are involved one way or another; if they are not a part of the cast, they usher, make costumes, make or collect props, handle sound or lights, bake cookies for intermission refreshments, or contribute to the thousand-and-one necessary details to put on such a production. We are very fortunate to have a professional director as a member of our choir and he does a masterful job as Director of our Variety Show. The Musical Director for the show is also an extremely gifted member of our church who freely gives of her talent and time. The highly-organized rehearsals begin immediately after the Christmas season and attendance is expected on Tuesday evenings and Saturday mornings. (This is in addition to the regular Thursday night rehearsal.) This is a demanding time commitment for the two or three months before the performances, but all agree that it is worth it!

The original purpose of the first Variety Show was to raise money for a choir tour to Europe. It was so successful that we have continued the production each year, long after our bags were unpacked and stored away. The show is always a great success; we raise money to give to a specific project, and it is a happy, shared experience for everyone. An additional BIG benefit is the outreach opportunity it provides for the entire congregation. We have people in our church who buy twenty, thirty, or forty tickets for their friends and neighbors. Many of these visitors have never been inside our church, and frankly, would not come to any church service, but they *will* come to our Variety Show. In a survey of our adult Sunday School classes, we learned that in almost every class there is at least one person, now a member, who first came to our church by receiving an invitation to the Variety Show. One of our ministers told us that the annual Variety Show is our church's greatest evangelistic outreach tool. This past spring, seven performances reached over 3000 people! After expenses, $10,000 was then available for our mission project. The investment of time and effort certainly did pay off.

Not every director is fortunate enough to have a choir with such a sweet, sweet charitable spirit. To us, it is quite amazing that in addition to their weekly singing and rehearsing (Thursday rehearsals go from 7:30-10 p.m.; Sunday morning from 8:45 a.m.-noon), they elect to dig deeper and donate money. And then they go even further, choosing to spend countless hours in rehearsals for the Variety Show. This really shows the level of their commitment to "serve the Lord with gladness!"

If you do not have such a group of singers who are also caring, loving people, may we offer a suggestion: the seed of charity must be planted by you. This is best done by an example of giving. Become a servant to your people. Call someone who needs a word of encouragement; send a card to someone who is ill; pick up a bag of groceries for a family in dire financial straits; take a choir member to lunch with no prescribed agenda other than to be a friend. We who are placed in the position of leadership must often take a look at our own attitudes and become aware of the needs of those we are called to serve. Leadership does come with a price tag:

For unto whomsoever much is given, of him
shall much be required . . . .
Luke 12:48

If we understand the position of "shepherd of the
flock" then our roles will be more clearly defined; we are
to live an example of giving. We have found this is best
accomplished one-on-one, rather than on a mass basis.
Seeing their director demonstrating an act of kindness
will do wonders to educate the choir in the fine art and
the full joy of giving. By His own actions, Jesus taught
his disciples how to love: feeding the hungry, clothing
the poor, and washing the dirty feet of exhausted travelers. Actions do speak louder than words!

Just as directors learn to get along with a wide variety
of choir people, so must choir members adjust to the
personality traits and foibles of their leader. We know a
lot of choir directors, and we can't think of any two who
are alike. You each have your own gifts, talents, personal
tastes, style, and demonstrate them in your own unique
way:

— some directors are highly organized, some create
chaos,

— some are volatile and outspoken; others
accomplish the same task by being calm and soft
spoken,

— some are musicians by birth; others are text-
book trained, some combine both,

— some love what they do; others regard it as "just
a job,"

— some encourage democracy within the choir; others are convinced that dictatorship is the only way to get anything done,

— some regard their spiritual leadership as being as important as their musical leadership; while others feel "that's the job of the pastor,"

— some have a preference for classical works; while other choose a steady diet of hymn arrangements or gospel songs.

The older we get the more we realize there is more than one way to travel down this road of life. Your *style* is not right or wrong, and it may not even be better than that of your peer across town, but it's *your* style. However, it is good that we can learn from each other. It is always helpful to discuss mutual problems, methods of administration, effective anthems, and to observe the rehearsals of others. A couple of hours spent watching another director at work might give you some terrific idea that will work with your choir. Quite often we welcome "visiting firemen" to sit at the side of our rehearsal room and watch us work on a Thursday evening. We appreciate watching others rehearse and perform. None of us can know everything there is to know about conducting, organizing a rehearsal, or inspiring a group of individual singers to blend and behave like a unified group. We need all the help we can get, and getting it from other directors is a great way to learn what to do or sometimes, what *not* to do.

FRED: Just as you bring your own expertise and personality to your position, I'd like to think that I do the same. With the hope that I can be helpful, I'll put myself on the line and share some Fred Bock theories. I'll divide these into four sections:

1. What to do prior to the choir season,
2. What to do prior to every rehearsal,
3. Running a smooth rehearsal, and
4. What to do before the next rehearsal.

Part 3

WHAT TO DO PRIOR TO THE CHOIR SEASON

Our choir season runs from September through June, and the Cathedral Choir sings almost every Sunday during these months. Having two months of summer vacation is a real boon to our music program. After serving faithfully for ten months of the year by singing Sunday services, memorizing anthems weekly, and rehearsing for the Variety Show and extra outside programs, these folks (and their director) are ready for some R & R. Burnout is minimal in our choir; having a long summer vacation is certainly a big help in maintaining everyone's desire to return in the fall. During July and August the Summer Choir sings each Sunday. The agenda for Summer Choir is less demanding and is a wonderful music ministry opportunity for folks whose busy schedules do not not permit them to be part of the Cathedral Choir. I am very fortunate to have a capable assistant who conducts during the summer months.

Every choir needs new members, and while some churches invite anyone who expresses a desire to sing to join the choir, we cannot. We are limited by space. Our choir loft is situated high above the main platform and pulpit. We are locked into a certain number of seats. Very few people leave our choir, so I do not have many "vacancy" signs posted on empty chairs in the loft. Therefore, I screen would-be choir members. This works to my advantage because I honestly prefer quality over quantity. I would probably not do well with a choir of hundreds of voices.

Have you ever envisioned yourself directing the "perfect choir?" I have! What would that be for you? My dream is to have a choir of about sixty-five voices with more men than women so that we can experience the full, rich choral sound that comes from a large men's section in a mixed choir. Once I had that vision, I started to build our choir in that direction. Let me suggest that such musical visualizations will help clarify your thinking and goals.

Recruiting new members for the choir can be done in several ways, but let me share one way of obtaining new men for the group. Every Father's Day the women in the choir get the day off because we have a Men's Chorus. This is done by open invitation. We have only one rehearsal following the second service on the Sunday prior to the performance. We get about forty new men: some who are teenagers and some who are octogenarians. This gives us a full loft of singing men who are joined by a nucleus of tenors and basses from the Cathedral Choir. It is quite a thrilling sound and the response from the congregation is overwhelmingly positive. The Men's Chorus has become a favorite tradition. We sing something easy, usually a unison, two-part, or very simple TTBB selection. When we sing our soft prayer response ending in a four-part chord with the basses singing a low F, it melts even the hardest heart! But I must admit that I have an additional ulterior motive in doing this. It gives me a chance to meet and to hear new men. Here's the trick: the men from the Cathedral Choir are not permitted to sit next to each other. They must sit next to one of our guests. This is hospitable, but they are also "auditioning" them! When rehearsal is over, my "choir-men-turned-spies" report to me if they have heard one who is a strong reader with an exceptionally good voice. (Now doesn't that sound like a plot right out of a Ian Fleming thriller?) I make a concerted effort to contact them about auditioning for me. This has been the single most effective choir recruiting idea I've ever tried. Other colleagues report similiar success in signing up men for their choirs. It just might work for you!

We have a women's chorus on Mother's Day with the same reception that we find on Father's Day. I use that opportunity to find out if there is a lady with a wonderful voice that we might be able to add to our choir. However, I must admit that I rarely need to recruit women. I seem to have more interested sopranos and altos then I do tenors and basses. I am told that's true in most churches.

I try to organize my choir season so that I have the same group from beginning to end. If I can solidify the choir membership by September 1, I can work with them and we will learn to grow together as a team without losing or adding new players every few weeks. I rarely, however, add new members during the choir season. I do like having new blood transfused into the existing body at the beginning of fall. These new men and women bring a sense of excitement, renewed energy, and a fresh vitality to our group. We can all use that!

I start planning for the fall season right after Easter. During the month of May a little announcement is put in the Sunday bulletin, stating that we are now taking applications for the fall choir season. When an interested party calls the music office, we mail an application form to be completed and returned to us. The application is very important because it not only gives the individual's musical background, but it also includes the applicant's personal testimony. This part of the application helps us separate those who are interested in being part of the choir for the right reasons from those whose motives seem questionable. It is always surpising to read some of the unacceptable reasons:

"I want a new social life."

"I want to appear on television," (our services are televised weekly — LET GOD LOVE YOU with Lloyd Ogilivie probably appears on a local station in your area.)

"I want to be part of a performing choral group."

"I need to get away from my kids one night a week."

"I've never been in a choir and I want to give it a try. I like new experiences."

Obviously none of the above reasons are poor ones, but they are not appropriate for our church choir. We are looking for men and women who want to use their gifts as a part of a service which leads people in worship and adoration of our Heavenly Father.

Here's what our application form looks like:

First Presbyterian Church of Hollywood
1760 N. Gower Street
Hollywood, CA 90028

MUSIC DEPARTMENT INFORMATION

Today's date:_____

Name _____ Home phone _____

Address _____ _____ _____
              Street   City   Zip

Occupation _____ Business phone _____

Birthday _____ Age: 20-35   35-5-   50-?

Are you a member of this church? _____ If not, what church are you a

member of? _____

Name of spouse, if married _____

Name(s) of dependents:

Outline of your past choral experience:

What part do you usually sing? _____

Have you had private voice training? _____ If so, state length of time and

teachers: _____

What instruments do you play? (well) _____

Check other interests:

Social _____ General Organization _____ Library _____ Mimeograph and

Reproduction _____ Poster and Art _____ Lighting and Electrical _____

Sound Systems _____ Publicity _____ I have good newspaper contacts _____

Entertaining _____ My specialty is _____ I know of available

musicians or entertainers _____ Other (please list) _____

_____

_____

List three individuals who know you well and could recommend you to serve in the Music Department with your talent. Members of this church would be highly preferable.

1. _____   _____
    name   phone

2. _____   _____

3. _____   _____

First Presbyterian Church of Hollywood is a dynamic and soundly evangelical church. Those involved in the Music Department's ministry are expected to support the goals and purposes of this church and to be open to growth in their own spiritual lives through the varied experiences of this department.

With this in mind, please prepare a brief, yet definitive statement of personal faith in Jesus Christ.

The next step is a personal interview in which I meet the applicant face to face. I try to encourage the perspective member to open up and share with me about his or her faith, vocation. hobbies, background, and introduction to our church. Then it is time for the musical portion of the interview, the audition. Most people really tense up for an audition. Friends of mine in the entertainment business tell me the same thing. No matter how many auditions they go on, there is a tenseness in every one of them. Remember that, directors, and keep in mind that when tense, applicants don't do their best work. I start the audition by asking the would-be choir member to sing, *Happy Birthday.* "Why, *Happy Birthday?* " you may ask. Well, for starters, everyone knows that song. And I like the octave jump in the middle. Hearing the tone quality on the low note and on the same note one octave higher gives me a better idea of the singer's range and the qualities of both the low and high register of their voice. I keep changing keys to see how far the vocal range will stretch and still sound good. We might do this song ten or twelve times before I know their exact range. Knowing this, I can determine if I have a potential I or II Alto or I or II Tenor, etc. Next, I invite the applicant to sing the melody of a familiar hymn. *When I Survey the Wondrous Cross* is a good one because it moves stepwise with no awkward intervals. When they have sung the melody, I have them sing the same hymn, only this time, sing their own voice part. I play all the other parts at the piano — but *not* theirs. This lets me know if they can hold their own without hearing their specific notes.

Next, I go to a hymn they probably do not know, and ask them to sight-read the melody. I play the chord of the key and their first note. They then sing *a capella* as far as they can. I give them three chances on each selection, but I never actually *play* their notes for them. I tell them verbally what their mistakes were, but I do not *play* the corrections. What I'm aiming to do here is get a choir of good readers, not good imitators! (Most every applicant tells me "I'm nervous, and that if I could just hear it, I would get it right!) Since we do so much music at rehearsals, we don't have time to hammer out every part of every song for each person to "get it"; hence the need for good readers.

Next I move on to anthems. I start off with a fairly easy selection and have them read their part. In all of this process, I tell them to forget about the words, just sing "oo" or "ah." Not being concerned about the words is one less thing for them to worry about. This gives me a better impression of their vocal quality which is not hindered by nervously having to sing the correct words. The "oo" or "ah" vowel sounds are generally more pleasant and listenable, and give a better impression of the applicant. I use three anthems: easy, medium, and difficult. Every once in awhile, I get an applicant who really does very well in this process. They like the challenge of sight-reading difficult music. These are the folks I really do want in my choir if for no other reason than to inspire the others! I am convinced that when much is expected, people *do* rise to the occasion. Having some super readers in the choir will make the others better readers.

The audition/interview is not over yet. When I've decided this is someone we need and want, I stress the need for their commitment. Being part of the choir is a special opportunity not to be taken lightly. We expect good attendance, punctuality, and participation in all rehearsals, performances, and the life of the choir. This is not the place for a person who will "come when he or she can," or will not come if he or she receives a "better offer." After a complete understanding of the responsibilities that come with being a choir member, if the applicant still wants to be a part of the group, we feel confident that it will be given a top priority. I strongly feel that the Lord deserves something better than a haphazard commitment!

Consequently, we have found that the folks we accept into the Cathedral Choir stay for a long time. We have one woman who has been in the soprano section for forty seven years. That's a record! Several have been there over thirty years. That's a strong commitment and a lot of notes sung! These are the people one needs at the core of a good choir. They inspire and challenge us all.

I try to complete the choir auditions by the end of June. By that time I know who will not be returning in the fall and what positions will be open, and I will then be able to fill those holes in each section. When the choir roster is completed, I go on to my other summer projects, namely selecting the music for the coming year and forming the master calendar.

Ministers in the Presbyterian church are given study leaves. Lloyd Ogilvie uses the month of July to prepare his plans, goals, topics, and sermons for the coming year. About the first of August, I receive a notebook which contains a comprehensive outline of the sermons for the coming year. He includes the basic theme for the series, the dominant theme for each sermon, scriptures and a few paragraphs describing what he hopes to accomplish each Sunday. Then my job is cut out for me: it is my responsibility to put together a cohesive service from the first note of the prelude to the last note of the postlude.

Here are some ways I go about that:

I make a master calendar for the year. I list all the communion Sundays, the Missions Sunday, the Stewardship Sunday, the New-Members Sundays, and all those out-of-the-ordinary days throughout the church year. If yours is a liturgical church or not, it matters little as there are special festive days in all our churches. While some may or may not celebrate Epiphany, we all celebrate Christmas, Easter, Palm Sunday, and Thanksgiving. Some celebrate Maundy Thursday, while others observe Good Friday. Many churches make a special commemoration of Mother's Day and Father's Day.

Then I fill in the dates where other choirs (the other adult choir, a smaller ensemble, one of our children's choirs, the teen choir, or one of our bell groups) or one of our soloists will sing. As you plan your choir year, now is the time to include as much as you can to avoid problems and disappointments when it's too late to change. However, I admit that at this point in my preparation I write everying in pencil — not ink!

I know that on any given Sunday we will need music for the following spots:

> Prelude
> Call to Worship
> Call to Prayer
> Hymns
> Anthem
> Offertory

Choral Benediction or Hymn
Postlude.

I begin this process by reading Lloyd's sermon outline, Scriptures, themes and explanation. When an idea hits me, I jot it down. After reading his themes for each Sunday from September through June, I begin the process of filling in the blanks. Then out come the files, books, boxes and stacks of anthems, responses, benedictions and hymns. Some of this is new material I have received and some of this is already in our library. During my travels if I hear an anthem that I like, I bring it back and put in a file marked "possibility" or into one marked "special day services." Then I have this at my disposal when I begin my music selection. I do my best to fit the music into the topics that Lloyd has prepared. Sometimes the ideas come quickly. Other times they require some research and real work to locate music that really does tie-in with the sermon content. Sometimes I am baffled. I recall one sermon where the text was "Behold, I will set a plumbline in the midst of my people Israel . . . " *(Amos 7:8).* Does *anyone* know an anthem that includes that text? That was the Sunday to sing a generic *Praise Ye the Lord* anthem!

August is a busy month around our house. I often consult that great resource book, *Catalog of Choral Music Arranged in Biblical Order,* by James Laster (Scarecrow Press, Metuchen, NJ), to help me find music on Scriptural texts from Lloyd's sermons. Through all this I keep my summer goal in mind: to have all the music selected, ordered, stamped, filed and ready to go by Labor Day weekend. So you see, I *have* to get my homework done. Before the season begins, it is always good to have as much planned and scheduled as possible. With the basics covered, fine tuning can then occur.

Another consideration is the degree of difficulty of the music I'm selecting. I need a broad spectrum here: some easy, some challenging. I keep in mind some practicalities: don't sing *a capella* eight-part anthems the Sunday after Christmas, Easter, or on Memorial Day Weekend. These are classic absentee days in the church music world. Do yourself a favor and schedule a rather easy selection for those days, one that will sound good with only 75 per cent of the choir present, and with a minimum of rehearsal.

I also try to include a wide variety of styles of music. If I schedule a piece by Bach, Mozart, or Beethoven, I make sure that the next week the anthem is *not* by one of those composers. I love the idea of being ecclectic in my musical choices. I often tell people, "If you don't like what we sang this Sunday, come back next week, because it will not be the same!" You might hear a Bach chorale this week, a Hank Beebe anthem next week, Mozart the following, John Rutter the week after, then followed by a William Dawson setting of a spiritual. Isn't that variety of music more fun for everyone — singers as well as listeners? I also like to plan a variety in accompaniment: organ, piano, piano with four-hands, *a capella,* oboe descant, violin, taped track. Even though we use these, I like to space them out over the year so that we don't fall into a rut of being predictable. What *is* predictable is that we are *un*predictable! That's what adds excitement to our worship expressions. And isn't that what part of our responsibilty is as directors of music to create an air of excitment about going to church? We do our part: by performing new pieces as well as old favorites, in a variety of styles, and then asking God to bless the creativity He gave us in the first place.

As I am putting together the music program for the year, I try to include a difficult work that I know will not "click into place" in one or two rehearsals. The choir needs to "grow into these" by stretching and working. Making this kind of demand will not win you a popularity contest the first time the piece is read. I can think of two pieces that we have done that are good examples of this growth: *Saul* by Egil Hovland, and *Jesus and the Traders* by Zoltan Kodaly. Both are not easy, and both contain choral writing that is especially effective, but demanding. *Saul* depicts the confrontation Saul had on the Road to Damascus, and the harmonic structures reflect the intensity of this encounter. *Jesus and the Traders* tells of Jesus' turning over the tables of those who sold sheep and doves in the temple; an equally distressing and harmonically clashing depiction. The choir hated both pieces from the start! But we stuck to it, working on only a few bars at first, and then we tried the first and last six to eight measures. After many rehearsals and lots of grousing from the singers, all of a sudden the tide turned and a few people started saying they might even like this piece after all. On *Saul,* the transformation that Saul experienced on that Road centuries ago took place in miniature the night at rehearsal when light struck us as well. The words, music, and meaning all came together at once. That year the choir voted *Saul* their favorite anthem. The same thing happened this past year with the Kodaly selection. I've tried presenting that piece three times, and this last time I vowed to myself that if I couldn't make it happen this time, I would personally take the responsibility of throwing away all 75 copies and never try it again. And this time — victory! The first two times we attempted this work, I got so discouraged that I quietly went through everyone's folders and removed it. Last fall when I brought it out again (hoping to have it ready for Palm Sunday, which is plenty of time if you start rehearsing it on Labor Day weekend!), it was met with the now-expected groans and "Oh-no, not-this-again!" reaction. However, I'm alive to tell the story that it pays to stick to your hunches. I suggest including a piece or two that will require hard work on everyone's part. The reward of rising to and meeting a challenge is a worthy goal. It certainly does help breed the "we can do it" attitude we want to cultivate in our choirs. It expands horizons and demonstrates to the choir and congregation that there are new ways of telling God's message. However, I would never put two such pieces back-to-back either in a rehearsal or in a service. That would not be wise planning.

I make notations on my copy of anthems as to which ones worked and which ones did not. I call them "repeaters" and "non-repeaters." I don't care to make the same mistakes twice.

The Prelude and Postlude are usually played by our wonderful organist, Kimo Smith, and he selects his own music. Occasionally we put one of our bell choirs in the Prelude spot. Sometimes we use both the bells and organ. During the Offertory spot, we may use one of our other groups or a soloist. So to add variety and interest to our weekly services I schedule these groups on the Master Calendar, knowing that everyone appreciates their performances.

As I read Lloyd's sermon outlines for the following year I try to be aware of what hymns are consistent with the themes of the sermons. The flow of a service can certainly be supported by the hymns. People love to sing the "old favorites." It is not best for a congregation to be force fed all new music, so bring out the new ones cautiously and not too often. During the course of the year Lloyd and I will spend time on the selection of hymns together for we have learned to go over every hymn a couple of weeks before the service to make sure that all the words fit the theme. We use only the verses that are appropriate for that specific morning's theme.

There are some additional organizational chores that need to be done before the choir season begins. We are becoming a society where our citizens are known by identification numbers rather than by name. I admit it is true in our choir room as well! When you become a member of a choir in our church you are assigned a number. That number is yours; your folder will have that number; it will be sewn into your robe, and your spot on the seating chart will be marked by that number. Our personnel chairperson is responsible for the number that will be yours. He or she will put your number on a 3" x 5" card which will also be color-coded. If you are a soprano, your color will be white, altos are green, tenors are yellow, and basses are salmon. We use a large peel-off black number that can be puchased at any stationery store. After your number and name are affixed to the card, we then laminate it. A hole is punched in the top so that it can be hung on our seating board, which is arranged in the same formation as our choir loft. When you enter the choir room, you will know immediately where you are to be seated. It's really a good system and one which adds to the efficiency of our department.

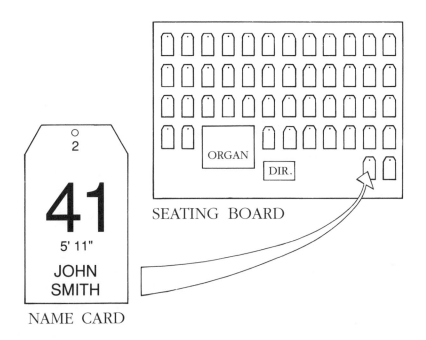

ranged in the same formation as our choir loft. When you enter the choir room, you will know immediately where you are to be seated. It's really a good system and one which adds to the efficiency of our department.

Putting each person's height on the card will help the personnel officer place the singers in a more uniform, orderly position. This can be a reminder not to put a 6'5" tenor next to a 4'11" alto.

Surely some of God's most saintly people are those who are our choir mothers and fathers. We have these for every choir in the church. They do a myriad of chores and give us a mountain of support. Our music program simply could not operate without them. They are responsible for making and serving coffee and refreshments, keeping the robes in good condition and order, acting as hostesses and hosts, removing spots from ties, mending emergency tears, dispersing aspirins, holding babies, and even disciplining the members of the younger choirs. These volunteers arrive before choir members, and are included in all social functions. They are loved as family members. They make my job easier and are a great encouragement to the entire music department. Do you have them? If not, I recommend that you seriously look for them within the membership of your church. I promise you, you'll never be sorry!

We've learned a lot of tricks of the trade from our librarians. Let me pass on some of their suggestions for your librarian. When new music arrives, it should be stamped with the church's name, address and your library file number. Stamp one copy DIRECTOR and another ORGANIST. These can then be put in a three-ring binder for easy use during rehearsals. The librarian places a little red peel-off dot on the spine of my copy and a yellow one on the copy for our organist. This makes these two copies readily identifiable in a stack of octavos. This is a small point, but when you're looking to find the Director's copy of an anthem, it will save you time.

Our librarians keep a card file of all of our music and the storage location where it is stored. We have each piece listed in two different files: a title file and a composer file. Listed on the cards are author, voicing, accompanied or unaccompanied, catalog number, publisher, and performance history. They also keep a record of any music loaned to another church, so that we can make certain it is returned to our library.

Several years ago when the hymnal, *Hymns For The Family Of God* (which I edited), was published, we ordered enough accompanist's editions so that we could take them apart for our choir. Our singers do not carry a hymnal into the choir loft. Each Sunday morning our librarians go to a file and take out the individual hymns that will be sung in the service. They are placed in the choir folders along with the choral music that the choir will sing. This makes their folders less bulky. At the end of the morning they are again placed in the file folders by hymn number, ready for use whenever that hymn is sung again.

All too quickly the summer is over and fall is here! For us, Labor Day weekend starts our fall choir season. For over thirty years the Cathedral Choir has used this holiday weekend as their three-day retreat. This "mini vacation" is not only for choir members, but also for their families as well. We host over 200 people at Carlsbad, California, where we stay at an Army-Navy Boys' Academy adjacent to the Pacific Ocean. While the accommodations are a bit on the Spartan side (you can say that again!) and the food is boarding school cafeteria style, it is a great place for the choir to kick off the new season. We have two retreats: this one where families join us and another one-day retreat late in January just for choir members. We find that the addition of spouses, children and friends to our weekend retreat is a wonderful idea. We have the opportunity to get to know each other's families on a social basis, and they get the opportunity to understand the ministry to which we feel called. Being invited to this retreat helps them to feel included in the music ministry, and they usually become very supportive of the family member who is in the choir. Let me remind you that being a spouse of a choir member does necessitate sacrifices. They do not get to sit with their husband or wife in church, Thursday nights are spoken for, and rarely do they get a weekend away. Having family retreats unifies us all. Choir kids meet other choir kids, and we can fellowship with friends involved in a common service to the Lord.

The schedule for the family retreat is a busy one, but includes plenty of opportunity for relaxing as well. We all attend chapel services; we all eat together, and the evenings are joyous times filled with parties and programs. Even the non-musical guests become involved in the evening's entertainment. The choir rehearses for about twelve hours, which gives us a real head-start on the music for the year. The retreat also helps newcomers to feel a part of the choir family, and we've devised fast and clever ways to make certain we all know who's who. The schedule of events for last year is included in the "Bonus" section to give you an idea of what goes on at our Labor Day Weekend Choir Family Retreat.

Another practical reminder: Before the choir season begins (and then again week after week), make sure the robes are clean and in good order (that's a job that is handled by our faithful Choir Mothers); do you have enough chairs, folders, pencils, music stands, Kleenex, paper clips, etc. for your choir's use? Get ready — here they come!

Part 4

WHAT TO DO PRIOR TO EVERY REHEARSAL

Articles II and III of our choir bylaws clearly state that attendance at rehearsals is very important. Members are *expected* to be at all rehearsals and performances. If they must be absent, they need to contact their Part Superintendent *prior to the rehearsal*. Anyone not at rehearsal on Thursday will not be allowed to sing on Sunday. With this kind of clear understanding between choir members and the Director, there should be excellent attendance at rehearsal each week. If we are going to do our best for the Lord, we need plenty of time together for instruction and practice. This needs to be understood and accepted by everyone.

My conviction is that our purpose in occupying the choir loft each Sunday is that of communication. For me, that means selecting the right music, be it a l6th century motet or a 20th century anthem — AND THEN DOING IT WELL. It must textually match the sermon and scripture, as well as be good music. Each piece should be rehearsed four to six weeks before the Sunday that it is performed. If it is to be memorized (and a great deal of our music is memorized), we suggest folks bring a small tape recorder and make a rehearsal tape to play in their car or home for a couple of weeks before the music is scheduled for a service. Listening to a rehearsal tape is a wonderful tool for achieving a better performance.

I do plan each rehearsal *before* the rehearsal. I don't "wing it" or "play it by ear." I try not to throw my choir members a curve during rehearsal. I list my complete musical agenda and include the dates on which the music will be sung. The choir members get their "Thursday Thing" when they pick up their music. They organize the music in their folders so that we don't have to waste time finding the next piece to be rehearsed!

Shown on page 107 is a sample of the "Thursday Thing." As you can see listed there are the myriad of announcements that seem to plague choir rehearsals as well as church services. We list as many announcements as we can on the "Thursday Thing" rehearsal bulletin. We also include birthdays to be celebrated that week and address and phone number changes. This saves valuable rehearsal time when announcements and information are printed.

My own personal style of handling a rehearsal is fairly laid back, but at the same time demanding. My personality is not one of emotional outbursts; therefore I am not the type to scream and yell. I would be uncomfortable with that technique. I may err at the other extreme. Because I have the desire to use humor in whatever way possible to keep people relaxed and attentive, I use it in rehearsals, too. Volunteer choir members are much more enthusiastic about coming to a rehearsal and giving it their best if they can laugh and have fun while they are doing it. Singers do sing better if they are not tense and nervous.

CATHEDRAL CHOIR

REHEARSAL SCHEDULE

November 4

Warm Up - Lou Robbins

Opening Prayer - Joy Foster

* means <u>memorized</u>!

386	*Let All the World	CTW	11-7
199	*Lord, Sanctify Me Wholly	CTP	11-7
423	*I Sing the Greatness of Our God	A	11-7
4th	All People that on Earth Do Dwell	Off	11-7
sheet	Praise to the Lord	Hymn Intro	11-7
380	*O Lord, Our God	CTW	11-14
2	*Great is Thy Faithfulness (p.7)	CTP	11-14
125	Jesus and the Traders	Palm Sunday!	
231	A Song of Praise	Off	11-21
239	*Sing and Rejoice (start p. 7)	CTW	11-21
312	*Lead Me, Lord	CTP	11-21
325	Salvation is Created	A	11-21
130	God Bring Thy Sword	A	11-28
390	O Sacrum Convivium	CommunionB	11-28
403	Tantum Ergo	CommunionW	11-28
414	*I Am the Light of the World	A	12-5

MusicNotes

1. We stay through <u>both</u> services on 11-28..Communion Sunday.

2. The new choir festival picture is framed and in place in the Hirt Music ROom. Those who ordered pictures, pick them up from Ken Hart.

3. Call for <u>this</u> Sunday is 8:45 am, robed and in place!

4. HAPPY BIRTHDAY this month to:
   Grant Matthews 11/4
   Patt Bennett 11/10
   Donna Hickox 11/12

5. All soloists, other directors, and Cathedral Choir officers: Please check your mailboxes in the Library. Some of these slots are jammed full and need to be emptied to-night! Thanks in advance for taking care of this.

Part 5

RUNNING A SMOOTH REHEARSAL

We *always* start the rehearsal on time and there are *always* half a dozen people who are consistently late, often the same ones, week after week. But I am there, and we start at exactly 7:30 with vocal warm-up exercises (which my soloists present very well), and prayer by the choir chaplain. Then I begin the actual music rehearsal.

Let's talk a little about vocalizes and warm up exercises. There are two purposes: one certainly is to warm up the vocal mechanism by singing scales and exercises that start in the middle section of the voice and gradually push it out in high and low directions. The second is to learn more about vocal production, correct breathing, posture and control for singing. By having a different soloist do this each week, we all learn more of the uniqueness of being a soprano, an alto, a tenor, or a bass. Together we are singing vowel sounds in these exercises that demand the same sound at the same time. The point is that when we apply this to our singing of choral litera-ture, we need to do the same thing! Sounds simplistic, doesn't it? But think of all the different ways you can say the word *Gloria.* Is it *Glow-ree-a, Glorr-ee-uh*...see what I mean? Here's the next trick; in your warmups, use intervals, and vowel sounds that are utilized in the pieces you are going to rehearse. Find the vowel sounds you want for Gloria, and make sure everyone is saying them the same way. When you rehearse that number, remind the folks how good it sounded in the warmup time. Make a practical application of what they did earlier in the warmup, making certain the connection is clear to the singers. Why don't I do the warmups myself? Why do I let others do them? They see me in action enough of the time. Having another person up front, in charge, helps them to appreciate others' interpretations and ideas. Using others also increases the team effort approach of our choir. It's not "me" and "them"; it's "us." Pinpointing the vocal problems and selecting the warmup exercises take time, but are well worth the effort.

Just after our break (which comes a little more than half-way through the rehearsal, so that the second half is shorter than the first half), the choir president presides over attendance reports from the section leaders as to who is absent, (and why!) and makes any other announcement that was somehow missed on the "Thursday Thing" choir bulletin.

We normally rehearse in the Hirt Music Room, our choir rehearsal area, but part of each rehearsal is held in the sanctuary choir loft. It helps to get the feel of the music we'll be singing the following Sunday in the sanctuary and to practice with the organ. (We only have a piano in the rehearsal room, no organ.) Before dismissal, we share prayer requests and praises, the choir chaplain closes in prayer, and we are usually on our way home by 10 p.m.

Often I will begin in the Hirt Music Room and then go to the sanctuary for the second half of the reheasal, or perhaps the other way around. Sometimes I will have the choir sit in sections, sometimes in quartets. I've even split the choir, or rehearsed in the round with all the sections mixed up. Use variety in your rehearsal time: don't be predictable! On a piece they know quite well, try having the choir seated in mixed quartet formation. First time around, seat them in twos . . . SSAATTBB-SSAATTBBSSAATTBB, etc. You will be amazed with the sound from your choir. And hopefully, they'll love it, too. Practice a few times in these positions so that they start to feel comfortable when seated this way. Being seated next to one other person from their section makes for a better sense of confidence in singing.

As the Director, I make all the selections of music and choose the people I want in the choir. The organization of the choir members is self-contained and democratic. The members report to each other and hold each other accountable for attendance. If anyone has more than two "unexcused absences" (the definition of that word varies with each excuse), then I will step in and either repri- mand, or in very few cases, dismiss him or her from the choir. That's the part I hate most about this job! I try to keep rehearsals relaxed and fun. Many of the people in our group have been gifted with wit and humor and have very few unexpressed thoughts! I like that kind of off- the-cuff humor and the freedom to share it. We allow those members the freedom to make us laugh. If rehears- als are not fun, musically challenging, and spiritually uplifting, we may lose valuable members. I don't want anyone leaving because rehearsals are dull! People sim- ply have too much to do these days to give up an eve- ning for something that is not rewarding. As choir directors, we must remember that we are working with a volunteer choir They have all put in a full day at their jobs *before we get them!*

If the music is not challenging, your best people will leave. As I mentioned earlier, try to select some music for the more musically advanced members, and the others will improve as you go along. Set high goals, and in most instances, people will rise to meet them. Good singers, who are good readers, become bored quickly with simple little melodies. Good singers do not want you to have to bang out the notes for the slower readers. Conversely, there's a danger in doing too much difficult music: as you will discourage slower readers. Establish a workable balance between "easy" and "difficult." (I prefer "readily accessible," and "challenging.") For extremely difficult works, we often have one section come early for a part rehearsal. Or, I divide the group and send each section to a different room in the church for a session of "banging out the notes." Sometimes wood-shedding is absolutely necessary to build confidence and to have the section sing with assurance. The section leaders or soloists (in our case that's one and the same) usually take the responsibility for these mini-rehearsals. Something can be said for keeping the musical expectation level rather high so that choir members will be stretched in their level of music reading, appreciation, and understanding. Everyone likes variety in the choir rehearsal. In your preparatory time, make sure you spread out the difficult pieces and intersperse them with some easier or more familiar pieces. Start off with a piece they know well so that they feel a sense of accomplishment right from the beginning. If you start with an octavo that requires extensive wood-shedding of parts, you'll put the choir in a "down" mood and they may not reach an "up" for the rest of the night! Scientists and psychologists tell us that just after the half-way mark lies the prime point of learning. Schedule your most demanding piece at that time to maximize your energies. Build to that point with pieces choir members will feel good about, and you will have prepared them well for the genuine work that lies ahead in the pieces that demand extra effort. I call this "successful programming for the rehearsal."

I want the rehearsals to go well so that everyone will feel comfortable and secure in the music we sing for the congregation. If singers have not been sufficiently re-hearsed, it will show on their faces and sound in their voices. Allow adequate time to rehearse a piece so that it feels solid with the singers. You'll need to judge by the degree of difficulty just how long to spend on each piece at each rehearsal. Nothing is deadlier than plowing through an anthem, missing notes all over the place, singing it over and over (and often with no explanation from the director as to why we should "do it one more time"), and then putting it away with a sense of accomplishing nothing. To alleviate that problem, you must determine when to start rehearsing a new piece. Most pieces require four to six weeks with my choir. If the work is not brand new and we have sung it within the last twelve to eighteen months, maybe two to three weeks would suffice. (Choir members forget what they've sung a lot quicker than directors!) Whoever said we have to rehearse all of every piece every week? If there's a tricky or demanding portion, rehearse that part only. I disagree with the concept of *constantly* going over the parts everyone knows well. Work on the sections everyone does *not* know well instead!

I go through my music before each rehearsal with those wonderful Post-it notes and list exactly what I want to accomplish in each selection. My notes might read "Altos, bar 3, page 7" or "men top of page 3." In the rehearsal, when we reach that piece, we waste very little time because I tell them we are starting on page 3 or page 7. Go directly to the problem. Solve it! Then go on to the next piece. The following week, go back to the same spot to remind them of the problem, check to see that they have not forgotten what they learned from one week to the next, and then come into it from a page or so earlier to cement it in place. Sing the *entire* piece occasionally with no need to run the entire piece week after week if it is already well-known, or presents no special problem to be solved.

If you have a one or a two-hour rehearsal, you need to determine for yourself just how long to spend on each piece so that you cover everything and do not arrive at dismissal time with four pieces you never opened. Looking over the repertoire, you can make an educated guess as to how long it will take you to accomplish what needs to be done. Write that guess on the Post-it note, and then take it one step further. Write down the actual time in the rehearsal that you should start this piece:

8:17 we start working on the alto entrance on
    page 4,

Jump over to the soprano line on page 5 that has
    that awkward leap in it ("Remember ladies

how we sang this interval in our warmup earlier this evening?")

Practice the *PPP* ending to make sure the blend is right, and check the balance between the unison women and the three-part men with the basses on a low "E".

All of that might take seven minutes, so we should be ready for the next title at 8:24, which we schedule for six minutes because we take a break for ten minutes at 8:30. If you do these exercises for awhile, you'll find that you don't talk as much in rehearsal, you sing more, and you accomplish more. Most of all, the singers feel rewarded, and you are a hero because obviously you have spent much time planning this valuable rehearsal. Believe me, they'll take note of your organizational efforts!

Lastly, always end on time. If you start on time and plan your rehearsals well, then there should be no reason why you can't also end promptly. My choir people get very antsy when we go beyond our dismissal time unless it's the week before a big concert. (Even then try to warn them that there is a possibility that they might need to spend an extra half-hour the next week. The more you let them in on what's happening, the better they will cooperate with you.) No one likes surprises when it means staying out extra late on a night he or she wanted to get home early! Some have to get home because of babysitters or young children and most of them have to rise early to go to work. We need to honor their private lives. I like to leave on time, too.

Before going home, however, I try to say a few encouraging words before the benediction prayer. A reminder from me as to *why* we are singing *what* we're singing (perhaps share how this ties in with the minister's sermon) makes the message of the anthem meaningful. We go home with the prayer that God will now take what we've worked hard to prepare and add the powerful touch of His Holy Spirit to our efforts, setting it free on wings to soar far higher than anything we ever hoped or dreamed. I often remind the choir that we are not entertainment; we're not a music concert society, and we're not here to promote anyone's musical tastes. We're here to minister and touch people's lives with the warmth and love of God Himself. That's a high calling, and that's why we spend hours rehearsing and doing our best.

Part 6

WHAT TO DO BEFORE THE NEXT REHEARSAL

After each rehearsal, usually when I'm driving home, I like to review and recall what went especially well and what we'll need to work on more specifically next week. At stoplights, I try to scribble down on a pad the selections I feel need some extra cleaning and polishing. As I think through the evening, there are usually things that pop into my mind that I wish I had said (sometimes there are things I wish I *hadn't* said) and I make note of those as well. If I don't know what it is I want from my choir, the choir will never know what to do to help me.

Then I question aspects of the rehearsal like the seating. Would the sound be better if I altered the seating pattern next week so that a voice that does not blend well is placed next to someone who does blend well.

Did the sequencing of the rehearsal move too slowly? Could the flow of the evening be improved by moving some selections for greater variety? How can I keep the element of freshness in the rehearsal?

Will the up-coming major concert require more than the ordinary amount of rehearsal? Should I include this into the rehearsal schedule?

I've found it effective to spend some time each week on a major work well in advance of the performance date. Perhaps some week when we are singing an easy anthem (do yourself a favor and program easy pieces into your schedule too), I will be able to afford to spend an hour on the major work. I do this early in the choir season so that the choir builds an enthusiastic love for the work and begins to understand the depth of its meaning.

And what about the accompanist? Do I need to spend some extra time on the accompanist's music before next week? I've learned that he or she needs to know well in advance if there is a piece with an especially demanding accompaniment. It's definitely not fair to throw a new piece with a million 16th notes that go like the wind, to the accompanist on the day of rehearsal with little or no warning! This makes the accompanist look foolish, and probably a little more than slightly angry for not being informed ahead of time! Occasionally, I will spend some time with our organist to go over some upcoming works and discuss tempos and registrations. If the accompanist knows what I'm after, then he can take the time necessary to prepare registrations, pistons, pedalling, etc., on his own.

Before you know it, it's time for the next rehearsal. As you start thinking of this style of organization, it will soon become second nature and you will be looking for ways to improve on yourself.

Even after you have done all that you know to do; you have selected the best music, organized the Music Department, planned your rehearsals, you must remind yourself that you will not please all the people all the time. We have to face the realities of life. Not everyone is going to be our best friend or even like us. Since we are human, we are susceptible to being hurt by relationships that never gel or ones which crumble for one reason or the other. Try to make amends, but if that doesn't work, go on and make the best of a painful situation.

At times we need to apologize and at other times we must confront a choir or staff member about his or her words or actions. That is never pleasant! Hopefully, after the air is cleared, healing can then begin and that is certainly necessary if we desire to build healthy relationships.

There are times when your role as leader means you become a mediator in the conflicts of others. Creating and restoring peace will further your goal of harmony within the choir. Just as you want to blend individual voices into a balanced choir, so you desire to meld the different personalities into a warm, caring family. That combination will reverberate harmony in your rehearsal room, in your church, and to the world.

Part 7

"THE BEST LAID PLANS . . . "

We've often thought a book of comical experiences that occur during church services would be a best seller. Even though the choir has spent hours rehearsing, ushers are trained to know where and how to seat worshippers, and the minister has done his homework by preparing a moving sermon, there are some Sundays where things can and do go wrong. In fact, it can be a nightmare come true in the light of day. When that happens, (and it will if it hasn't already,) just make the best of it and go on. We invite you to laugh with us.

A few Sundays ago our 9:15 service started with a joyous Call to Worship for the hundreds of early risers who were there to greet the Lord's day. Then it seemed that everything fell apart. It was a *busy* service including reception of new members, plus all the usual elements in the order of worship. Our first problem began with the illness of the Head Usher and a substitute was called. During the time of receiving new members, a lady sitting in a pew near the rear of the church, had a heart attack and the paramedics had to be called. That emergency was executed beautifully with almost no commotion or noise. Our minister, in a masterful way, stopped the service and prayed for this woman. The ushers were a little confused by this time and made the mistake of taking the offering at the wrong time — during the choir's anthem! HeavenBound (our teenage choir) was supposed to sing immediately following the offering, so like they had been instructed, they stood and proceeded to the lower platform. Their director is a member of the Cathedral Choir, so she left the choir loft in a hurry, changing from her choir robe to her director's robe as she ran down the steps at the fastest possible speed. When she reached the door leading to the front of the sanctuary, she found it had inadvertently been locked. Meanwhile, the organist, seeing the choir members in place naturally thought their director was in her place as well and gave the introduction to their anthem. And the teens, not knowing what else to do, went ahead and sang — perfectly! She stood outside the locked door thinking, "How can they be singing — I'm out here!" It was certainly to her credit that she had prepared those teenagers to be so poised in the face of such a dilemma.

Several years ago the choir under a previous director lost their customary decorum within the first few minutes of the service. The Cathedral quartet sits in four theater type seats in the center front row of the choir loft. They and the choir had filed in ceremoniously, properly carrying their folders in their left hands. When the director gave the cue to sit, they did so in beautiful precision. Except the back of the alto's chair suddenly broke, tossing her backwards with her feet straight up in the air, in full view of the congregation. She was retrieved from her embarrassing position and went right on with the service as if nothing had happened. What a trouper! The choir, however, had a difficult time being retrieved from their giggles into an attitude of worship.

From time to time we have had little cherubs who are part of a children's choir fall from their perches on the platform or go to sleep in their seats waiting the cue to stand and process to their singing position. Nothing can bring smiles to the faces of our congregation like the antics, mistakes, and devilish behavior of our little angels.

One of our favorite mishaps was at the end of a wonderful, inspiring solo. The bass stood on the platform beside a tall, white wicker, cone-shaped basket of lovely spring flowers. His final note, a rich low G, vibrated right into the hearts of those in attendance and right to the center of the floral arrangement causing it to fall forward down the steps and splash all over the floor. It was a much bigger finale than he anticipated, and snickers could be heard from every corner of the sanctuary.

Two years ago we had all the combined choirs performing Robert Russell Bennett's "The Many Moods of Christmas". Since our loft only holds about 65 singers, we used the lower platform and the fronts of both sides of our U-shaped balcony as extended choir lofts. On the right side sat the children's choirs. As Fred was conducting the Cathedral Choir in the loft, a very polite, but very nauseous little girl pushed her way to the front row to ask the director's permission to leave. However, her timing was more *adagio* than *allegro,* and her lunch and dinner ended up on the floor and pews of the front balcony — again in full view of all the other children, and the audience as well. But the children, being children, were not terribly gracious about the sight and smell. Holding their noses, they all clutched their robes and hastily moved away from the spot where their embarrassed friend stood. Since Fred was so occupied conducting, the entire drama went unnoticed by him. His first realization that something unusual was going on was when a church custodian came through the front door carrying a mop and a bucket. Fred's immediate reaction was stifled anger — "Why in the world would that custodian choose this time to mop the sanctuary floor?" Needless to say, the laughter only added to the festive mood.

You could probably relate just as many humorous or disastrous happenings within the walls of your church. We'd love to hear them sometime to add them to our growing file of "When best laid plans fail, then revert (or backslide) to laughter!"

Chapter IV

HARMONY IN YOUR OWN FAMILY

Keeping Personal Relationships in Tune

HARMONY IN YOUR OWN FAMILY
or
KEEPING PERSONAL
RELATIONSHIPS IN TUNE

The only certainty about the church music world is that there is no perfect mold or formula for the participants. Choir Directors come in all shapes, sizes, and colors. Some are single, many are married, with or without a family. They possess a multitude of gifts and have a supply of friends. We don't want to overlook any of you. We are smart enough to know it would be impossible to discuss adequately every emotional need of every music director. High school creative writing teachers usually tell their students to write about what they know. Even though we are not trying to get a grade for this "term paper," we are still going to take that advice. Since we Bocks are family people, with twenty five years experience in marriage and twenty one years experience in parenting, we are going to direct some of our thoughts to the problem of balancing our church responsibilities with the role and the relationships of family. It is our hope that some of our words will be applicable to those of you who are single.

Since no one is an island, we can all learn a little about getting along with others by learning about family relationships. You may find that what we have to say about families is helpful in dealing with family members in your role as a leader at church. If you don't live with your biological family, any of these ideas can be adapted to your extended family or circle of friends. *All relationships require time and effort;* we'll share some thoughts on how to make them more meaningful and fulfilling. Mr. Webster[1] tells us that one definition for the word *harmony* is:

> a combination of parts into a pleasing, orderly whole.

That is a goal for our lives — to put all the parts together into a pleasing whole. Our ministry, our choirs, our jobs, our staffs and our families are all better served if we can establish this harmonious combination. Relationships, outside of music and work, need to be developed and nutured. Dr. Archibald D. Hart says in *15 Principles for Achieving Happiness:*

> There is little disagreement among researchers on what produces happy people; they seem to agree about almost everything. Above all, however, there is very strong agreement that happiness is produced by having close relationships, especially friends on whom one can depend. The unhappiest people of all are those who have no friends.
>
> It is human nature that one can never be deeply and abidingly happy until we give ourselves in love to others. As we sow the seeds of love we reap the joy of a rich happiness harvest.

> (p. 147)[2]

---

1 Garden City, NY, Doubleday and Co., 1967
2 Dallas, TX: Word Publishing, 1988

Indeed, it would be a sad, unfulfilled person who could somehow establish a thriving music program, build happy, harmonious relationships within the church, and not be able to do the same in his or her personal life.

When our marriage was new and we had yet to embark on the uncertain journey of parenthood, some friends in the South introduced us to a pretty teenage girl. Her blue eyes mirrored a deep inner hurt and bitterness. Talking with Elaine (not her real name), we soon learned some of the reasons for her anger as her reservoir of pain began to spill freely. She began by telling us she planned to leave home just as quickly as she was legally of age. She seemed more than a little anxious to escape her parents' home and to live on her own. She went on to explain that her relationship with her father, who was a senior minister of a rather large church, was one of constant friction. With a defiant, piercing stare, she shared how the church had robbed her of her father. He left the house early each Sunday morning and didn't arrive home until long after the benediction for the Sunday evening service. She was not welcome in his office and was told not to bother him on Sundays because of his obligations to his parishioners. The rest of the week he served as the chief administrator of the church, called on the sick, chaired elder or deacon meetings, kept his staff happy, and was much too tired from his exhausting schedule to be of any earthly good to his family. He was away several evenings a week for committee meetings or obligatory social events. On his list of priorities, his wife and children came last. Yet, he enjoyed the reputation as a caring pastor, but he did not have the same treasured reputation at home! Elaine grew to feel that every person in the world was more important to her dad than she was. She had lived sixteen years with a painful feeling of rejection by the man who was so busy being a pastor that he didn't take the time to be a daddy. One comment jarred us, *"When I leave home, I will never again have to go to church and believe me, I won't!"*

Several months ago, we were with these same friends. We inquired about Elaine and were told that she had indeed left home at a young age, had unsuccessfully pursued several careers and had experienced two broken marriages. With a total lack of understanding, her dad feels that Elaine represents a big personal disappointment. She rarely sees her parents and never attends church. She proved to be a person of her word.

Some conversations stay with you forever. That early exchange with Elaine is one of them. We have never forgotten Elaine and the terrible pain she felt. Since our lives are so involved in the church, surrounded by what seems like an army of people with an arsenal of problems, we are doubly aware of the risks we take with our own children. Early on, we decided to put our family at the top of our priorities and allow them to have an active part in our lives. We try to put their needs before the needs of the rest of the world. Our children are important to us and we want them to feel valued. We chose to keep an open door in the music office, even on busy Sundays, and to make our children feel welcome to come in to see us any time. On many Sundays, not only will you find our sons in the office, but you might also find an assortment of their friends there as well. (It is good for our humility to remind ourselves that ours is the only office in the church to have a tray of donuts on the coffee table. There is something more than our personalities to entice our children!) We do not want our boys to feel in any way that the church has deprived them of their parents. In fact, the opposite has happened with our sons, Stephen and Jonathan. We were on the staff of Bel Air Presbyterian Church at the time of their births. They were welcomed into this world not only by their biological family, but also by the choir family. Immediately our children felt love and acceptance at church. Very early in their lives, it became one of their favorite places to be. Why not, when you can get so much affection and attention from a group of adults! That collection of choir singers became their extended family. When we left Bel Air to move on to Hollywood Presbyterian Church, again the choir and Music Department became their "family." Isn't that the way the church should be? As parents, we feel so very grateful to these two choirs for helping us raise our boys. As teenagers they have a sense of ownership in our music program. For them, it is a home away from home. They enjoy being involved at church. Unlike Elaine, Stephen and Jonathan are anxious to *be* at church, not anxious to *leave* it.

Since there is no tried-and-true method of raising successful, well-adjusted, spiritual children, you may think that we have a great deal of audacity to write about our own family. In no way are we trying to set ourselves up as examples for you to follow. We are not. We merely want to share our observations from years spent in the "church business." In doing so, we willingly make ourselves vulnerable to your scrutiny. That seems extremely risky because we know that we have not been perfect people or perfect parents. Our boys are far from perfect offspring (even though they may try and convince you otherwise). As a family, we have our share of disagreements and disappointments with each other. There are times when those all-too-typical sibling arguments are heard loudly in our home, but we hang in there together, each of us knowing that we are committed to one another. We try to resolve conflicts and arguments right away and not let the sun set on situations where people are upset. Forgive, forget, and move on, assuring the people involved that our love and concern for them does not change. We are determined to help each other grow and to be held accountable to the other members of the Bock family. Should you see our imperfections, please be kind and remember to "Be patient, for God isn't finished with us yet."

We believe God uses "significant others" in the lives of children and teenagers. Very often, when children need support and love from those outside their immediate families, you and I can be the person to help a child in his or her spiritual growth. Friendships developed in the choir can easily give children of choir members access to the kind of help they need at various stages of their growth.

We love to watch people. We have learned from their mistakes as well as their successes. We've learned to be bold enough to ask questions and wise enough to ask for advice from those who have traveled this road before us. We've observed the interaction between parents and children, and we often sit back in awe at the skill that is used by some mothers and fathers. One family that has held our attention for several years is that of Dr. and Mrs.

Ponder Gilliland and their grown children. Their daughters and son have always enjoyed an open door policy even though they have grown up in a pastor's home. One story that has been passed on to us concerns their youngest daughter, Sheri, who was a student at the local high school in Oklahoma City. One afternoon she called her dad's church office, asking to speak with him. His secretary informed her that he was in a meeting, but if her question was very important, she would interrupt him. Sheri assured her that the question was very important, and that "my dad would want to talk to me." So the secretary put the call through.

Sheri was writing a paper and couldn't remember how to spell a pertinent word and knew that her dad would know. Her father did know how to spell the word, but what is more important, he knew how to make his young daughter feel valued enough so that she felt the freedom to call him at any time, understanding that she would get through to him and gain his full attention.

Sheri later told the secretary what she wanted, and the secretary said, "Why Sheri, I could have spelled that word for you." But Sheri said, "But I knew my dad would really know how to do it." Today Sheri is a young businesswoman who has a vital walk with God. She understands that the love and acceptance she receives daily from her parents is only a small token of the love that God has available for His children.

As church workers, we easily become so engrossed in doing worthwhile tasks, that we neglect the people who should be the most important to us and who rightfully feel that we are the most important to them. It may not be very comforting to know that all of us can be replaced at our work, but let us remind you that we *cannot* be replaced in our own home. We sometimes remind ourselves of the old adage, *"It is the good that robs the best."* Adopting the bad habit of letting our "good" (all those services, committee meetings, conferences, business meetings, early morning study groups) robs us of the "best."

FRED: Because of the many professional hats that I wear, I somehow found myself working seven days a week. It didn't alarm me because my family often spent some of those working hours with me and I was having a wonderful time. After an extremely busy summer touring Europe with our church choir and conducting choral workshops around the United States and Canada, Lois found herself with the sensation of drowning in the whirlpool of constant activity. She shared this sense of depression and malaise and said she felt she simply had to have some time alone with me without a crowd of people around us. My original response was, "What do you mean? We see each other a lot!" In the days that followed, I began to understand what it was she wanted and needed. Facing myself honestly, I had to admit that my ego was being fed by my public appearances. However, those appearances did not meet the emotional needs of my family. I had to listen to Lois' requests. One thing I have come to understand about myself is that no matter how altruistic it may appear, no matter how pure my motives and purposes may be, my own personal ego is fed when I am conducting a choral workshop or leading the choir on Sunday mornings. If you will be honest, I'm certain that you will come to a similar conclusion. It requires effort on my part to make sure that my own ego needs do not cloud my thinking or become the driving force behind my decision-making.

After a few days of discussion, we decided to take Tuesdays off. In the beginning this was met with some reluctance on the part of the male member of this partnership, but it has proven to be the best thing we could have done for our marriage. Somehow the same amount of work gets finished with one less day in the office. This sacrifice became a wonderful gift to us both. We don't think we could exist without our Tuesdays together. (Part of why we chose Tuesdays was that on most Tuesdays the boys are in school and we can be alone!) We would honestly feel cheated now without our special time together. Sometimes we have little one-day outings away from the city; frequently, we go out to lunch, and then there are the days when we simply work in the yard or clean out the garage. But we do it together and hopefully alone.

LOIS: I, too, found myself over-booked with activities and meetings. I didn't realize how the world was taking chunks out of our relationship to each other and to our children. When I recognized my own needs and found that Fred was agreeable to taking the time to be with me, I made a decision never to take any appointments or invitations on Tuesdays. I love Tuesday; it's the best day of the week!

We know couples, and you probably do too, who pass like ships in the night. Sadly, many of these folks serve on a church staff. They work hard in very demanding jobs and go in opposite directions most of the time. Often, some will wake up to find that they no longer have a close relationship. They simply share a roof over their heads and mutual bills to pay. If this empty and unsatisfactory arrangement is allowed to go on, then a "point of no return" occurs. Marriage deterioration means that one or both partners no longer care. When that point comes, it is often too late to retrieve and re-build the relationship. Like Humpty Dumpty, all the king's horses and all the king's men can't put the pieces of such a marriage back together again. Before that happens, we urge you to examine your priorities and values. Dr. Dorothy Corkhill Briggs states, "the opposite of love is not hate, but indifference." *(Your Child's Self Esteem: The Key to His Life)*[3] Indifference to each other can mean that you simply do not recognize or value the other person's needs.

The people we value need our attention, time, and love to build a foundation for growth and security. When blocks of time have been reserved for another, that very act demonstrates how special that person is to us. It is impossible to build a healthy relationship when one member does not feel cherished.

Family relationships as well as friendships are like fertile seeds which need to be nurtured and cared for in order to grow. There is no effective way to sustain that love with someone who is special to you if you refuse to invest yourself and your time in the relationship. Without

---

3   Garden City, NY, Doubleday and Co., 1967

time, the necessary foundation will erode and a gigantic chasm will be carved in the underlying soil. A lack of time communicates indifference and thereby builds a wall of rejection, one brick at a time. These bricks are made from many statements: "I'm really sorry I can't spend time with you, but I'm so behind in my work," or "I've had to call an officers' meeting to deal with the budget, so I'll have to cancel our plans," or "I've got to meet with my staff to go over the selection of music so I'll have to shorten our time together." Put enough of those bricks together and you'll find you have constructed a huge wall, sealing out the very people who mean the most to you.

Let us share some specific ways that we have learned to avoid this problem:

From time to time, block out definite time on your calendar to spend with your family and friends. We have found that this planned time varies as our family constantly changes with different school and activity schedules. When our boys were younger, we kept Monday evenings as our family time. We did a variety of activities on those evenings, from planned lessons to picnics, from picking out a show we'd all enjoy, to attending Dodger games or eating at a favorite restaurant. It didn't really matter *what* we did as long as we did it *together*. We found this built good self-esteem in our children, because they learned that they were important enough that we cleared our calendars just for them. Never once did our boys ask to be excused from a planned family time.

We learned quickly that these times were not times to be used for disciplining or scolding. These were times for celebrating our family and for encouraging each other.

These times were not to be spent watching television (except during the World Series, since we are all baseball fans.) During the World Series, we would often plan a meal of hot dogs and Cokes, eat around the coffee table in the family room, and cheer on our favorite team (Our cheers are really loud if one of the teams playing happens to be the Dodgers!). Normally we feel that television is a poor family activity because it does not require or stimulate any active participation or conversation. You can be totally passive watching television, learning next to nothing from each other as you sit in front of the screen.

One of the greatest joys a family can share is reading aloud. From the pages of a book, you all make the same friends, share the same thrilling adventures, and learn the same lessons. What an exciting summer we had when we read C. S. Lewis' *The Chronicles of Narnia*. How we wish we could relive those weeks with our young sons. Aslan became one of our most beloved fictional characters, and all of us learned the lessons of right *vs.* wrong and light *vs.* darkness. Many times, we would plan to read just one chapter, only to come to the end with family cries of "Don't stop now — keep going!" We have amassed a great wealth of shared experiences and treasured memories. It is a deposit that we can draw on at any time!

> 'I know well that only the rarest kind of best in anything is good enough for the young.' Childhood is so brief and so open and formative. Impressions are taken into maturity. I cannot believe that children exposed to the best of literature will later choose that which

is cheap and demeaning. That is why only the
best is good enough for children, for we are
shaping a future.

(Gladys Hunt in
Honey for a Child's Heart)[4]

Establish the discipline of praying together as a family.
Several years ago we began keeping a prayer journal. As
we share our requests with each other, we write them in
a notebook. This ordinary notebook has become our
very own spiritual history book. When we are troubled
about a problem, we find instant encouragement in re-
reading this book to see how God has answered our
prayers in the past and helped us work through some
dark times. We realize that God cares about us as individuals and as a family.

Create a sense of shared ministry and mission in the
family. A parent's job at church will not seem like a
threat to a child if he or she understands and shares the
purpose of the work. If the family members can be in
agreement as to the reason they worship and serve in a
church on Sunday morning, have rehearsals on Thursday
nights, visit a friend in the hospital, or attend a committee
meeting on Monday night, the force of their resentment
will usually dissipate. Communicate with the family as to
what it is that you do in your work — let them know
when the rehearsals are fun (or a drag), that "Sue Jones"
needs our prayers and thoughts, or that the budget committee is having a very important meeting next Monday
to see if they can afford a full orchestra for the Christmas
concert. Keep them informed as new developments

---

4   Grand Rapids, MI, Zondervan Books, 1969

occur. You will find that your family will take a genuine interest in your work, if you use these skills of communication.

Just as we treat those outside the family with good manners, so do our families need to be the recipients of our kindness. Send your spouse and children a hand-written letter or card (for no special reason other than to tell them you love them) to help them feel valued. Everyone likes to receive personal mail, even your family members. The United States Postal Services can be used to express your gratitude, pride and love to a family member. You will find that there is no better way to use a postage stamp!

Celebrate your family. If you don't do it, no one else will do it for you. Let's face it. We live in a dark world and the daily news makes it seem darker all the time. But there are rays of light across the darkness, and they are the love of God for us and our love for others. Each family is unique and special. Discover together what that uniqueness is and what makes you special: traditions, hobbies, likes, dislikes, vacations, interests, friends, memories and faith. Your family deserves and needs the joy and happiness you can build into their lives by an investment of your time, love and guidance.

We can be on a church staff and still have strong, caring, personal relationships with our family and friends if we simply take the time to harmonize with the people who are a special part of our lives.

> "Finally, all of you, live in harmony with one another; be sympathetic, love as brothers, be compassionate and humble."
>
> *I Peter 3:8*

CODA

A Musical P.S.

A MUSICAL P.S.

Whether serving as a minister of music is your chosen vocation or your avocation, you are many things to many people: conductor, musician, spiritual leader, administrator, employee, employer, spouse, parent, child, and hopefully, a perennial student of music, spiritual truth and life. This is a pretty large order to fill! Does all of that make you want to pull the covers over your head and not face the day? Do you feel rundown, exhausted, lacking joy and purpose? If you say yes to these questions, then you need to put on the brakes right now and come to a screeching halt! You need time to evaluate your life, your goals, and your activities. In other words, it's time to regroup!

There is no successful way to take on a busy schedule and meet heavy demands without some kind of organization. For some, organization is easy, but for others it is next to impossible. Some people seem to be born with a great supply of neat and orderly genes. They always seem to be in total control, while others spend most of their lives trying to catch up to the rest of the world. Over the counter in a local Tarzana (that's our hometown) store, there is an amusing sign that catches our eyes every time we shop there:

Your lack of planning does not necessarily
constitute an emergency for me!

How often does our lack of planning constitute an emergency for someone else? We have been guilty of creating chaos from time to time. It is a battle we must always fight.

We all know people who have enormous gifts but whose talents are buried under the stack of missed appointments, unanswered mail, unreturned phone calls, chaotic homelife and the inability to change those habits and life-long patterns. If this sounds all too familiar and you feel unable to lift yourself out of the rut you have created, why don't you seek someone else's advice, — maybe from a book or a seminar. Plenty of books have been written on time management, and there are classes offered all the time at local colleges to help you put your life in order. Trained counselors are eager to assist in your quest for a more productive life. A friend of ours often reminds us that time management is simply *self-management*. We all need to organize ourselves better to accomplish the great deeds God wants us to do.

Have you ever noticed that the one personality trait in those who seem unable to cope with life's demands is that they are always the victim in life? Feeling they accomplish very little, they never give their family and friends the time they need. Often they are late paying bills. Usually their work is mediocre at best; they then take the only way out by blaming their circumstances on someone else's actions. It's time to stop playing the role of victim and become a *victor!* Of course, if you *enjoy* being the victim because it affords you attention and sympathy, then you are indeed "standin' in the need of prayer" and probably some counseling too!

Our lives and schedules can be self-destructive if we let them. Wouldn't you feel better about yourself with some positive re-enforcement? How many of you are reading this and saying, "I don't have the time or energy to change," or "I can't seem to get myself going." If these are your problems, then seek some help. Perhaps a good friend or a fellow staff member might be able to listen and then to suggest how to extricate you from that all-engulfing mire.

FRED: For some reason it seems that it is more difficult for a man to seek help or counsel than it is for a woman. There are probably many reasons for this; many of us were trained to be silent and never admit that we have problems. And some parents have done a very effective job of teaching their sons to repress their true emotions *unless it is that of anger*. Let's allow our emotional computers to be re-programmed. Admitting defeat and looking at ourselves honestly does not mean that we are less manly. It simply means that we are not afraid to admit that we are human and can use some assistance.

For those who are so organized that your schedule becomes your top priority in life rather than a tool to serve you and others, may we suggest that you mix into your agenda some ingredients of tenderness, flexibility, caring, love, and listening. Are you so super-organized that you treat interruptions to your planned schedule with annoyance? Have you stopped believing people are more important than schedules and plans? Let's remind ourselves that interruptions and disappointments are often really disguised opportunities. Recently, our minister, Lloyd Ogilvie, used an illustration of the Chinese script symbol for the word "crisis." It is two characters side by side: one indicating disaster, wrapped around the other which symbolizes opportunity. In our lives we must somehow learn to juggle:

plans and people,
sleeping, eating, and exercising,
worshipping, and working.

Are you open to consider some helpful hints that we have gleaned from the harvest of some time-management experts? Here goes:

Have a plan. Without one, you will never reach your goals— because you have none. Write your goals down right here in this book:

Ten-year goals _____

Five- year goals _____

One-year goals _____

One-month goals _____

Weekly goals _____

Daily goals _____

Hourly goals _____

If you do not own a weekly or daily planner, run, do not walk, to your nearest stationery store and buy one. In our family, Lois always has her constant companion, a well-worn grey DAY RUNNER, while Fred keeps his EXECUTIVE'S WEEKLY MINDER open on his desk. We both like to make lists of things to do, people to call, letters to write, items to buy. We find it rewarding to mark off the accomplished tasks. (Fred accomplishes much by creating a list of things to do which includes some things he's *already done* and crossed off the list! From the word go, he feels good about his agenda! That's because he's a wee bit crazy!) We have learned not to be too hard on ourselves; we don't make our expectations too great. Not *every* item has to be checked off *every* day. If things are left undone, we simply put them on tomorrow's list. Post-it notes put on mirrors, dashboards, the door to the garage, the phone, and even the refrigerator are reminders to all of us; part of our effort to maximize what we do in one day. We know people with wonderfully organized and compartmentalized minds who never seem to forget anything. Not true of Fred or Lois! A mildly depressing thought is that as we grow older, the more we need to rely on our lists and our reminder notes. Is that senility? Hope not!

Most of our friends owned telephone-answering machines long before we did. I guess we had some "hang-up" about them. A family member gave us one for Christmas a couple of years ago, and now we don't know how we ever lived without it. It saves so much time! We often keep it on while we are at home working and check it every hour or so for messages. Many times friends or associates leave a message, and a return call is not necessary. It is a wonderful tool to help avoid spending hours on the phone each day. Another must in being well-organized is to return phone calls promptly. If nothing else, it clears your conscience. Besides, it is freeing *not* to have all those unanswered calls hanging over your head. Of course, it's simply good manners, a way of showing others that they are important by promptly returning their calls.

Writing letters used to be an important part of people's lives. Today, we live in such a mad, hectic world that we don't allow ourselves the time, energy or creativity it takes to express ourselves on paper. Letter writing is a splendid, but seldom-used skill. It is a skill that requires time. Studying history is much more interesting today because our forefathers and mothers took the time to write not only their thoughts, their advice, their gratitude and sympathy, but also to chronicle the events in their lives. Aren't you glad that the Apostle Paul was thoughtful enough to write letters? Don't you think he was probably an organized person? Since the days of the Ephesians, Philippians, and Galatians, it seems that just about everyone loves to get letters, and yet, most of us procrastinate about answering or initiating letters. Since we love to get letters, why is it so easy to put off *writing* them? Not Fred! Believe it or not, he answers almost all mail the day it arrives. He also encourages his staff to do the same. It may work at the office, but he has yet to succeed with his wife. (She is trying, however.) Doesn't it make a lot of sense to answer an inquiry quickly, making it a one-step procedure, rather than a three-or-four-step procedure? Think about it for a minute. If you receive a letter that must be answered, you first open it;

then you stack it on top of the other mail to be answered; then you move the stack from the table to your desk, possibly to a drawer or file. Eventually, you must spend your day answering that mountain of mail. Ho-hum! Often, when you continue to collect letters to be answered, you find that you have missed a deadline, an important event, or the deep need of a friend who was counting on you. Simply put, not answering letters, as well as not returning phone calls, is rude. As Christians, we need to make every effort to be polite and considerate, honoring the needs of our fellow human beings.

Another comment we would like to make is that we have noticed a few people, yes, even some people in the ministry, who have an attitude of, "Well, since I'm in the Lord's work, I've got some perks coming to me." This means that they receive these gifts, not with a grateful heart, but rather with a sense of using others. They expect discounts from businesses in the community and freely rendered services by people in the church. A person who has these kinds of expectations often does not give of himself or even adequately expresses gratitude. We know one person who never acknowledges gifts received. He does not believe in writing thank-you notes or even picking up the phone to say thank you. His attitude takes the fun out of giving gifts to him. While he may feel thanksgiving in his heart for all that he has received, he has never developed the common courtesy of expressing it. Maybe he always means to, but he just can't get organized enough to do so or just can't be bothered.

Maybe his prayer and ours should be:

O Lord, give one thing more! Give to us a grateful heart.

Let us make every effort to see that our lack of gratitude, our lack of organization, and our lack of manners, do not become a hindrance to the Gospel of Jesus Christ. Let's use every possible positive means to let people see Jesus in us.

Keeping our lives "well oiled" with organization, manners, courtesies, spiritual commitment and growth, while getting along with our choirs, staff, ministers, family, and congregation is truly living in harmonious accord in a world that is rife with chaos. We have a marvelous reason to do so!

For several years we have had a simple, little framed picture hanging by our back door. It is a drawing of a bird with a caption that reads:

> A bird does not sing because he has an
> answer, he sings because he has a song!

As Christian singers and choir directors, we not only have a song, we also have an answer. It is an answer for a society that desperately needs to hear God's song. This divine Singer has a message of love, forgiveness, grace, and hope. He has asked us to be an instrument of His communication. We are indeed blessed and honored with such a high calling.

His mandate for us is:

> Sing because you have a song and *the* answer!

146

BONUS SECTION

How to Make Your Choir Sound Better—FAST!

Fred's 101 Favorite Anthems

Suggested Inspirational Reading

"The Church Musician and The Copyright Law"

HOW TO MAKE YOUR CHOIR SOUND
BETTER — FAST!

These ideas are not all my own. I am certainly indebted to teachers, friends and colleagues whose ideas I've "borrowed" over the years.

Some of these suggestions might sound simplistic, and indeed, some of them are simple ideas, but I have found all of them to immediately improve the sound of the choir. Even your choir members will notice the improvement right away.

Make certain that the singers learn to take full, deep breaths as they sing. Have a rehearsal room that is well lighted and properly ventilated. And (this is really basic), make sure that each person can see the director!

Check to see that everyone is pronouncing the words the same way. Consonants of the words should be sung together rhythmically...especially the final consonants of t,k,d,z, and s. (S is the worst sound in the world, and if just one hasty singer puts the final 's' on a word too soon, everyone will notice!)

Maintain the same positions of the lips, tongue, chin, and shoulders whether singing loudly or softly. We tend to constrict the sound when it is supposed to be soft. Maintain the same supportive energy and pressure from the diaphragm. Otherwise the sound will sag and go flat. Practice singing the same four-bar phrase loud, medium-loud, medium-soft, soft, and softer. The choir should be able to hear the difference when sung with energy rather than sung casually and unsupported.

Defy the natural tendency of singing louder the higher you sing. Instead, as you sing higher, sing softer and lighter to avoid a vocal quality that sounds "pushed."

Inspire your singers with a solid, full explanation of the text. The words carry the message of the music. Challenge your choir to match whatever emotional qualities are called for in the text with their singing voices. The text is the inspiration for the music.

Take control of the vibrato situation. Your choir needs to know that an out-of-control vibrato has no place in choral singing. Practice singing a well-known hymntune with full (and perhaps overdone) vibrato. They will laugh at how this sounds. Then sing the same hymntune with absolutely no vibrato whatsoever: a pure, straight tone. Next, strike a happy balance with the sound you want from your choir, somewhere between these two extremes. In some cases, choirs have no idea of what kind of a sound you want them to make. Some will need constant reminding to control their vibratos.

Remind your choir not to sing so loudly that they cannot hear the people on either side. If a singer cannot hear the person on the right or the left, then he or she is singing too loudly!

Singers need to maintain good posture for singing whether standing or seated (feet flat on the floor, please).

Music folders need to be held so that the music can be read and the director seen *at the same time*. Often heads get buried in choir folders, chins are dropped, and the sound of your choir changes dramatically — and for the worse. Work on this aspect of choral posture.

I hope these thoughts help you and your choir make a better choral sound as well as a joyful sound to the Lord!

FRED'S 101 FAVORITE ANTHEMS

General Anthems

ALL THAT HATH LIFE AND BREATH
PUBLISHER: MARK FOSTER
RENÉ CLAUSEN

ALLELUIA
PUBLISHER: E.C, SCHIRMER
RANDALL THOMPSON

AWAKE, MY HEART
PUBLISHER: H.W. GRAY
JANE MARSHALL

BEST OF ROOMS, THE
PUBLISHER: E.C. SCHIRMER
RANDALL THOMPSON

COME, LET US SING
PUBLISHER: SHAWNEE PRESS
GIOVANNI GABRIELLI

DEEP RIVER
PUBLISHER: WALTON
ARR. NORMAN LUBOFF

E'EN SO, LORD JESUS, QUICKLY COME
PUBLISHER: MORNINGSTAR
PAUL MANZ

FESTIVAL TE DEUM
PUBLISHER: GENTRY
FRED BOCK

GAELIC BLESSING
PUBLISHER: OXFORD
JOHN RUTTER

GIVE ME JESUS
PUBLISHER: AUGSBURG
ARR. L.L. FLEMING

GLORIOUS EVERLASTING
PUBLISHER: BRODT
THOMAS COUSINS

GOD BRING THY SWORD
PUBLISHER: BOOSEY & HAWKES
RON NELSON

GOD IS OUR REFUGE AND STRENGTH
PUBLISHER: HOPE
ALLEN POTE

GREAT LORD GOD, THY KINGDOM SHALL ENDURE!
PUBLISHER: THEODORE PRESSER
GEORGE F. HANDEL

HOLY IS THE LORD
PUBLISHER: GENTRY
FRANZ SCHUBERT

HOW EXCELLENT IS THY NAME
PUBLISHER: BOURNE
EUGENE BUTLER

I LIFT UP MY EYES TO THE HILLS
PUBLISHER: HOPE
ALLEN POTE

I LOVE THE LORD
PUBLISHER: HINSHAW
HANK BEEBE

I SING THE GREATNESS OF OUR GOD   FRED BOCK
    PUBLISHER: FRED BOCK MUSIC CO.

IN THE SHADOW OF HIS WINGS   KEN MEDEMA
    PUBLISHER: RON HARRIS MUSIC

KYRIE ELEISON (from SOLEMN MASS)   LOUIS VIERNE
    PUBLISHER: MARK FOSTER

LAST WORDS OF DAVID, THE   RANDALL THOMPSON
    PUBLISHER: E.C. SCHIRMER

LEAD ME, LORD   SAMUEL WESLEY (ARR. FRED BOCK)
    PUBLISHER: FRED BOCK MUSIC CO.

LET ALL THE WORLD IN EVERY CORNER SING   ROBERT BAKER
    PUBLISHER: H.W. GRAY

LIGHT OF THE WORLD, THE   PAUL SJOLUND
    PUBLISHER: WALTON

LORD BLESS YOU AND KEEP YOU, THE   JOHN RUTTER
    PUBLISHER: HINSHAW

LORD IS MY SHEPHERD, THE   THOMAS MATTHEWS
    PUBLISHER: H.T. FITZSIMONS

LORD, SANCTIFY ME WHOLLY   JEAN PASQUET
    PUBLISHER: H.T. FITZSIMONS

MAJESTY AND GLORY OF YOUR NAME, THE   TOM FETTKE
    PUBLISHER: WORD

MORNING STAR, THE   PAUL SJOLUND
    PUBLISHER: WORD

MY ETERNAL KING   JANE MARSHALL
    PUBLISHER: CARL FISCHER, INC.

NEW 23RD, THE   RALPH CARMICHAEL
    PUBLISHER: LEXICON MUSIC

NONE OTHER LAMB   CRAIG COURTNEY
    PUBLISHER: BECKENHORST PRESS

NOW SING WE JOYFULLY UNTO GOD   GORDON YOUNG
    PUBLISHER: SHAWNEE PRESS

O LORD, OUR GOD   OVID YOUNG
    PUBLISHER: GENTRY

O LOVE THAT WILL NOT LET ME GO   JOHN NESS BECK
    PUBLISHER: BECKENHORST PRESS

ON EAGLE'S WINGS   MICHAEL JONCAS
    PUBLISHER: N.A.L.R.

ONE HUNDRED FIFTIETH PSALM, THE   HOWARD HANSON
    PUBLISHER: CARL FISCHER, INC.

PRAISE HIS HOLY NAMES   FRED BOCK
    PUBLISHER: FRED BOCK MUSIC CO.

PSALM 148   GUSTAV HOLST
    PUBLISHER: GALAXY MUSIC

SAUL   EGIL HOVLAND
    PUBLISHER: WALTON

SECRET OF CHRIST, THE   RICHARD SHEPHERD
    PUBLISHER: ROYAL SCHOOL OF CHURCH MUSIC

SING AND REJOICE   WILL JAMES
    PUBLISHER: H.T. FITZSIMONS

SING MY SOUL, HIS WONDROUS LOVE   NED ROREM
    PUBLISHER: C.F. PEETERS

SING UNTO GOD   GEORGE F. HANDEL
    PUBLISHER: CARL FISCHER, INC.

SING WE MERRILY   SYDNEY CAMPBELL
    PUBLISHER: NOVELLO (THEODORE PRESSER)

SWEET, SWEET SPIRIT   ARR. ALAN DAVIES
    PUBLISHER: FRED BOCK MUSIC CO.

THANK THE LORD   RENÉ CLAUSEN
    PUBLISHER: MARK FOSTER

THANKS WE GIVE   DALE WOOD
    PUBLISHERS: CHORISTERS GUILD

WE HAVE COME TO WORSHIP YOU   C. HARRY CAUSEY
    PUBLISHER: FRED BOCK MUSIC COMPANY

YE SHALL GO OUT WITH JOY   HANK BEEBE
    PUBLISHER: HINSHAW

YE SHALL GO OUT WITH JOY   JOHN NESS BECK
    PUBLISHER: KJOS

Standard Repertoire

GLORIA IN EXCELSIS   W.A. MOZART
    PUBLISHER: G. SCHIRMER

HALLELUJAH! (MT. OF OLIVES)   LUDWIG BEETHOVEN
    PUBLISHER: G. SCHIRMER

HOW LOVELY IS THY DWELLING PLACE   JOHANNES BRAHMS
    PUBLISHER: G. SCHIRMER

IF YE LOVE ME, KEEP MY COMMANDMENTS G. SCHIRMER	THOMAS TALLIS
JESU, JOY OF MAN'S DESIRING PUBLISHER: G. SCHIRMER	J.S. BACH
LET THY HOLY PRESENCE PUBLISHER: FRED BOCK MUSIC CO.	PETER TSCHESNOKOFF
O, HOW LOVELY PUBLISHER: H.T. FITZSIMONS	ANTON BRUCKNER
OMNIPOTENCE, THE PUBLISHER: G. SCHIRMER	FRANZ SCHUBERT
PRAISE THE LORD IN HIS HOLY PLACE (SAB) PUBLISHER: GENTRY	L. LEWANDOWSKI
SHEEP MAY SAFELY GRAZE PUBLISHER: GALAXY	J.S. BACH

Hymn Arrangements

ABIDE WITH ME PUBLISHER: FRED BOCK MUSIC COMPANY	ARR. LUCY HIRT
ALL PEOPLE THAT ON EARTH DO DWELL PUBLISHER: LAWSON-GOULD	ARR. FLORENCE JOLLEY
CANTICLE OF FAITHFULNESS PUBLISHER: HOPE	ARR. DAN BIRD
COME YE FAITHFUL, RAISE THE STRAIN PUBLISHER: HINSHAW	ARR. FRED BOCK
COME, YE THANKFUL PEOPLE, COME PUBLISHER: FRED BOCK MUSIC CO.	ARR. PAUL SJOLUND & FRED BOCK
HOLY FESTIVAL, A PUBLISHER: FRED BOCK MUSIC CO.	ARR. JOHN NESS BECK
I NEED THEE EVERY HOUR PUBLISHER: BECKENHORST PRESS	ARR. JOHN NESS BECK
JOY TO THE WORLD, THE LORD IS COMING! PUBLISHER: FRED BOCK MUSIC CO.	ARR. FRED BOCK
KUM BAH YAH PUBLISHER: HINSHAW	ARR. PAUL SJOLUND
LIFT HIGH THE CROSS PUBLISHER: CONCORDIA	ARR. CARL SCHALK
MY FAITH LOOKS UP TO THEE PUBLISHER: HINSHAW	ARR. PAUL SJOLUND

O FOR A HEART TO PRAISE MY GOD   ARR. FRED BOCK
    PUBLISHER: FRED BOCK MUSIC CO.

PRAISE GOD!   ARR. FRED BOCK
    PUBLISHER: SACRED MUSIC PRESS

PUT ON THE WHOLE ARMOUR OF GOD   ARR. JOHN NESS BECK
    PUBLISHER: BECKENHORST PRESS

THOU ART GOD!   ARR. JOHN NESS BECK
    PUBLISHER: BECKENHORST PRESS

UPON THIS ROCK   ARR. JOHN NESS BECK
    PUBLISHER: G. SCHIRMER

WHEN I SURVEY THE WONDROUS CROSS   ARR. GILBERT MARTIN
    PUBLISHER: THEODORE PRESSER

Advent—Christmas—Epiphany

HE CAME HERE FOR ME   RON NELSON
    PUBLISHER: BOOSEY & HAWKES

HODIE, CHRISTUS NATUS EST   MARY E. CALDWELL
    PUBLISHER: GENTRY PUBLISHING CO.

HOSANNA TO THE SON OF DAVID   DANIEL MOE
    PUBLISHER: THEODORE PRESSER

I LOOK FROM AFAR   ANTHONY PICCOLO
    PUBLISHER: ROYAL SCHOOL OF CHURCH MUSIC

JOYFUL ALLELUIAS   JOHN WEAVER
    PUBLISHER: BOOSEY & HAWKES

NOW IS BORN THE DIVINE CHRIST CHILD   ARR. ROGER WAGNER
    PUBLISHER: LAWSON-GOULD

PEACE, PEACE   RICK & SYLVIA POWELL
    PUBLISHER: FRED BOCK MUSIC CO.

SING WE NOW OF CHRISTMAS   ARR. FRED PRENTICE
    PUBLISHER: GENTRY

THOU SHALT KNOW HIM WHEN HE COMES   HAL HOPSON
    PUBLISHER: HAROLD FLAMMER

THREE KINGS, THE   HEALEY WILLAN
    PUBLISHER: OXFORD

Lent—Palm Sunday—Easter

AN EASTER SYMPHONY   ARR. MILTON RUSCH
    PUBLISHER: FRED BOCK MUSIC CO.

CHRIST IS RISEN   JAN SANBORN
    PUBLISHER: FRED BOCK MUSIC CO.

CHRIST IS RISEN   PAUL SJOLUND
    PUBLISHER: WALTON

DAY OF RESURRECTION, THE   THOMAS MATTHEWS
    PUBLISHER: H.T. FITZSIMONS

HOSANNA TO THE SON OF DAVID   DANIEL MOE
    PUBLISHER: THEODORE PRESSER

JESUS, BORN TO DIE   ALLAN PETKER
    PUBLISHER: FRED BOCK MUSIC CO.

PROCESSION OF PALMS   MALCOLM WILLIAMSON
    PUBLISHER: G. SCHIRMER

QUANDO CORPUS MORIETUR   GIOVANNI ROSSINI
    PUBLISHER: GENTRY

REQUIEM (CANTATA)   GABRIEL FAURE
    PUBLISHER: H.T. FITZSIMONS

SERVICE OF DARKNESS (CANTATA)   DALE WOOD
    PUBLISHER: HAROLD FLAMMER

WITH THE WAVING OF PALMS   FRED BOCK
    PUBLISHER: FRED BOCK MUSIC CO.

Communion

COME SHARE THE LORD   BRYAN JEFFERY LEECH
    PUBLISHER: FRED BOCK MUSIC CO.

COME TO ME   CRAIG COURTNEY
    PUBLISHER: FRED BOCK MUSIC CO.

TAKE, EAT   FRED BOCK
    PUBLISHER: FRED BOCK MUSIC CO.

TANTUM ERGO   WILLIAM MATHIAS
    PUBLISHER: OXFORD

THERE IS A REDEEMER   MELODY GREEN
    PUBLISHER: SPARROW

UBI CARITAS   MAURICE DURUFLE
    PUBLISHER: EDITIONS DURAND (THEODORE PRESSER)

SUGGESTED INSPIRATIONAL READING

A DAY AT A TIME   DICK HALVERSON
     PUBLISHER: COMPCARE PUBLISHERS

A DIARY OF PRIVATE PRAYER   JOHN BAILLIE
     PUBLISHER: CHARLES SCRIBNER & SONS

A LONG OBEDIENCE IN THE SAME DIRECTION   EUGENE H. PETERSON
     INTERVARSITY PRESS

A MUSICIAN LOOKS AT THE PSALMS   DON WYRTZEN
     PUBLISHER: ZONDERVAN

A TESTAMENT OF DEVOTION   THOMAS R. KELLY
     PUBLISHER: HARPER & ROW

ADVENTURES IN PRAYER   CATHERINE MARSHALL
     PUBLISHER: BALLANTINE BOOKS

ANGELS   BILLY GRAHAM
     PUBLISHER: WORD, INC.

BORN AGAIN   CHARLES COLSON
     PUBLISHER: SPIRE BOOKS

CALVARY ROAD   ROY HESSION
     PUBLISHER: CHRISTIAN LITERATURE CRUSADE

CELEBRATION OF DISCIPLINE   RICHARD J. FOSTER
     PUBLISHER: HARPER & ROW

COME BEFORE WINTER   CHARLES SWINDOLL
     PUBLISHER: MULTNOMAH PRESS

COUNT IT ALL JOY   BARBARA JOHNSON
     PUBLISHER: BAKER BOOK HOUSE

DIFFERENT DRUMS   M. SCOTT PECK
     PUBLISHER: TOUCHSTONE

DISCIPLINES FOR THE INNER LIFE   BOB BENSON
     PUBLISHER: WORD, INC.

EIGHTH DAY OF CREATION   ELIZABETH O'CONNOR
     PUBLISHER: WORD, INC.

ESCAPE FROM REASON   FRANCIS SCHAEFFER
     PUBLISHER: INTERVARSITY PRESS

FIFTEEN PRINCIPLES FOR ACHIEVING HAPPINESS   ARCHIBALD D. HART
     PUBLISHER: WORD, INC.

GOD CALLING   RUSSEL
     PUBLISHER: SPIRE BOOKS

GOD UNLIMITED   NORMAN GRUBB
    PUBLISHER: CHRISTIAN LITERATURE CRUSADE

GOD'S BEST FOR MY LIFE   LLOYD JOHN OGILVIE
    PUBLISHER: HARVEST HOUSE

GUIDEPOST DAILY DEVOTIONAL   VARIOUS
    PUBLISHER: FOUNDATION FOR CHRISTIAN LIVING

GUIDEPOST MAGAZINE   VARIOUS
    PUBLISHER: FOUNDATION FOR CHRISTIAN LIVING

HIND'S FEET ON HIGH PLACES   HANNAH HURNARD
    PUBLISHER: LIVING BOOKS

HYMNS FOR THE FAMILY OF GOD   FRED BOCK, EDITOR
    PUBLISHER: BENSON PUBLISHING

KNOWING GOD   J. I. PACKER
    PUBLISHER: INTERVARSITY PRESS

LETTERS AND PAPERS FROM PRISON   DIETRICH BONHOEFFER
    PUBLISHER: THE MACMILLAN COMPANY

LIFE TOGETHER   DIETRICH BONHOEFFER
    PUBLISHER: HARPER & ROW

LIFESIGNS   HENRI NOUWEN
    PUBLISHER: DOUBLEDAY CO.

MAKING ALL THINGS NEW   HENRI NOUWEN
    PUBLISHER: WALKER AND COMPANY

MERE CHRISTIANITY   C. S. LEWIS
    PUBLISHER: MACMILLAN COMPANY

MY UTMOST FOR HIS HIGHEST   OSWALD CHAMBERS
    PUBLISHER: DODD, MEAD & CO.

NOW AND THEN   FREDERICK BUECHNER
    PUBLISHER: HARPER & ROW

ONE YEAR BIBLE
    PUBLISHER: TYNDALE HOUSE PUBLISHERS

ORDERING YOUR PRIVATE WORLD   GORDON MAC DONALD
    PUBLISHER: THOMAS NELSON

PARALLEL BIBLE
    PUBLISHER: TYNDALE HOUSE PUBLISHERS

PEOPLE OF THE LIE   M. SCOTT PECK
    PUBLISHER: TOUCHSTONE

PRAISING AND KNOWING GOD   HARDY AND FORD
    PUBLISHER: WESTMINSTER PRESS

PRAYERS   MICHEL QUOIST
    PUBLISHER: SHEED & WARD

REACHING OUT   HENRI NOUWEN
    PUBLISHER: DOUBLEDAY CO.

RESTORING YOUR SPIRITUAL PASSION   GORDON MAC DONALD
    PUBLISHER: THOMAS NELSON

SCREWTAPE LETTERS   C. S. LEWIS
    PUBLISHER: BARBOUR AND COMPANY, INC.

SIT, WALK, STAND   WATCHMAN NEE
    PUBLISHER: TYNDALE HOUSE PUBLISHERS

SPACE FOR GOD   DON POSTEMA
    CRC PUBLICATIONS

SPIRITUAL LEADERSHIP   J. OSWALD CHAMBERS
    PUBLISHER: MOODY PRESS

TEACHING A STONE TO TALK   ANN DILLARD
    PUBLISHER: HARPER & ROW

THE CHRISTIAN'S SECRET OF A HAPPY LIFE   HANNAH W. SMITH
    PUBLISHER: FLEMING H. REVELL

THE CHRONICLES OF NARNIA   C. S. LEWIS
    PUBLISHER: THE MACMILLAN COMPANY

THE CHURCH AT THE END OF THE 20TH CENTURY   FRANCIS SCHAEFFER
    PUBLISHER: GOOD NEWS PUBLISHERS/CROSSWAY BOOKS

THE COST OF DISCIPLESHIP   DIETRICH BONHOEFFER
    PUBLISHER: THE MACMILLAN COMPANY

THE GENESEE DIARY   HENRI J. M. NOUWEN
    PUBLISHER: IMAGE BOOKS

THE GREAT DIVORCE   C. S. LEWIS
    PUBLISHER: THE MACMILLAN COMPANY

THE HIDING PLACE   CORRIE TEN BOOM
    PUBLISHER: WORLDWIDE PUBLICATIONS

THE KNOWLEDGE OF THE HOLY   A. W. TOZER
    PUBLISHER: HARPER & ROW

THE MAN IN THE MIRROR   PATRICK M. MORLEY
    PUBLISHER: WOLGEMUTH & HYATT, PUBLISHERS, INC.

THE MASTER PLAN OF EVANGELISM   ROBERT COLEMAN
    PUBLISHER: FLEMING H. REVELL

THE MYTH OF CERTAINTY   DANIEL TAYLOR
    PUBLISHER: WORD, INC.

THE PROPHET   KAHLIL GIBRAN
  PUBLISHER: WALKER AND COMPANY

THE RADIANCE OF INNER SPLENDOR   LLOYD JOHN OGILVIE
  PUBLISHER: UPPER ROOM

THE ROAD LESS TRAVELED   M. SCOTT PECK
  PUBLISHER: TOUCHSTONE

THE SACRED JOURNEY   FREDERICK BUECHNER
  PUBLISHER: HARPER & ROW

UNWRAPPING SPIRITUAL GIFTS DAVID ALLAN HUBBARD
  PUBLISHER: WORD, INC.

UP WITH WORSHIP   ANNE ORTLUND
  PUBLISHER: REGAL BOOKS

WALKING ON WATER: REFLECTIONS ON FAITH AND ART MADELIEN L'ENGLE
  PUBLISHER: HAROLD SHAW PUBLISHERS

WHEN THERE IS NO MIRACLE   ROBERT WISE
  PUBLISHER: REGAL BOOKS

WHISTLING IN THE DARK   FREDERICK BUECHNER
  PUBLISHER: HARPER & ROW

WITH CHRIST IN THE SCHOOL OF PRAYER ANDREW MURRAY
  PUBLISHER: SPIRE BOOKS

YOU GOTTA KEEP DANCIN'   TIM HANSEL
  PUBLISHER: DAVID C. COOK PUBLISHING CO.

YOUR GOD IS TOO SMALL   J. B. PHILLIPS
  PUBLISHER: WALKER AND COMPANY

THE CHURCH MUSICIAN
AND
THE COPYRIGHT LAW

PRELUDE

On October 19, 1976, President Gerald R. Ford signed into law Public Law 94-553 setting forth the law of the land in regard to copyrights. This new law became effective January 1, 1978.

GUIDELINES for the use of copyrighted music material

These guidelines do not presume to be a comprehensive summary of the Copyright Act of 1976. It does not attempt to deal with all the issues covered by the legislation, nor does it provide answers to many of the legal questions.

It is intended to be a guide to understanding the nature of copyright by the users of church music to improve their ministries, to maintain a proper standard of ethics, and to help protect themselves and their churches from incurring liability or subjecting themselves to the possibility of being embarrassed or even sued. The questions addressed are the ones which are most frequently asked by church musicians.

A complete copy of the Copyright Law of 1976 and further information regarding the Copyright Law may be obtained by writing: The Copyright Office, Library of Congress, Washington, DC 20559.

1. WHAT DOES "COPYRIGHT" MEAN?

Our nation's founding fathers determined that it was in the public interest that the creative works of a person's mind and spirit should belong, for a limited time, to the creator. The protection of these

161

works is called "copyright." The United States Copyright Law grants to any copyright owner the exclusive rights to original materials for a term which is *equal to the length of the life of the author/creator plus fifty years.* (For many songs written prior to 1978, the term is 75 years.) The copyright owner is the only one who has the privilege of reproducing the work. If any other party wants to reproduce the material in some manner, permission must be obtained from the copyright owner.

Visible notice of copyright should appear on all copies of a copyrighted music. Whether on the owner's original works of on permitted copies, the notice should be visible and contain the word "copyright" or the symbol (for printed material) or (for sound recordings), the year of first publication and the name of the copyright owner.

2. WHAT ARE THE RIGHTS OF COPYRIGHT OWNERS?

A. To reproduce the copyrighted work in printed copies or on records, tapes, video cassettes, or *any duplicate process* now known or which later comes into being.

B. To make arrangements and adaptations of that copyrighted law.

C. To distribute and/or sell printed or recorded copies of the work or to license others to do so.

D. To perform the copyrighted work.

E. To display the copyrighted work.

3. WHO OWNS THE LEGAL RIGHT TO MAKE COPIES?

The original creators (authors and composers) and/or publishers, assigned agents, etc.

4. DO OTHER COUNTRIES HAVE COPYRIGHTED LAWS?

Yes. Most of the world now seems to recognize the need to give incentive and protection to creative persons. Copyrighted material owned by U.S. citizens is protected in many other countries by these countries' copyright laws and treaties with the United States.

5. WHAT IF I'M FACED WITH A SPECIAL SITUATION?

If you want to include copyrighted lyrics in a song sheet . . . arrange a copyrighted song for four baritones and kazoo . . . or make any special use of copyrighted music which the publisher cannot supply in regular published form, the magic word is . . . *ASK.* You may or may not receive permission, but when you use someone else's property you must have the property owner's consent.

6. WHAT IF THERE'S NOT TIME TO WRITE?

Think of copyrighted music as a piece of property, and you'll be on the right track. *Plan ahead.* Some publishers routinely grant permissions over the phone.

7. WHAT ABOUT PHOTOCOPIES OR TAPES THAT ARE NOW IN OUR CHURCH?

Immediately destroy any unauthorized photocopies, tapes, etc., and replace them with legal editions. Possession of any illegal copies puts you in the position of harboring stolen goods.

8. IS IT PERMISSIBLE TO:

- TAKE A PHOTOCOPY OF A COPYRIGHTED WORK FOR MY ACCOMPANIST IN ORDER TO SING A SOLO?

- PRINT WORDS ONLY OF A COPYRIGHTED WORK ON A ONE-TIME BASIS FOR USES SUCH AS CHURCH BULLE-TINS OR SONG SHEETS?

- PRINT SONGBOOKS OR SONG SHEETS CONTAINING COPYRIGHTED WORKS AND USE THEM IN CHURCHES, BIBLE STUDIES, OR HOME PRAYER GROUPS AS LONG AS THEY ARE NOT SOLD?

- MAKE A TRANSPARENCY OR SLIDE OF A COPYRIGHTED WORK FOR USE BY PROJECTOR?

- MAKE COPIES OF COPYRIGHTED MUSIC FIRST AND THEN ASK PERMISSION?

NO. Permission must be secured prior to any such uses and/or duplications.

9. WHAT IF I CAN'T FIND THE OWNER OF A COPY-RIGHTED SONG, CAN I GO AHEAD AND USE IT WITH-OUT PERMISSION?

NO. Check the copyright notice on the work, and/or check with the publisher of the collection in which the work appears. Once you know the name of the copyright owner, write or call the Church Music Publishers Association at the address on page 165 for assistance in locating an address or phone number. For a cost reimbursement of $2, CMPA will supply a current listing of major sacred music copyright holders/publishers. Please send cash. CMPA cannot invoice.

10. BUT WHAT ABOUT ITEMS THAT ARE OUT OF PRINT?

Most publishers are agreeable, under special circumstances, to allow reprinting of out-of-print items; but, again, permission must be secured from the copyright owner prior to any duplication.

11. WHAT IS PUBLIC DOMAIN?

If a song is in the public domain (P.D.), the copyright protection for the song has expired and the song is dedicated to the public for use as it sees fit with no permission being required from anyone. The absence of a copyright notice (see question 1) is one indication that a song may be P.D.

12. WHAT IS FAIR USE?

Fair Use is not generally available to churches. Fair use is a doctrine developed by the courts which permits portions of copyrighted works to be legally reproduced for purposes of criticism, comment, news reporting, classroom teaching, scholarship, and research. In no instance does this apply to a performance. The various interest groups involved have agreed upon guidelines which constitute the minimum and not the maximum standards of educational fair use. If you are interested in a copy of these guidelines, please contact CMPA at the address on page 165 and enclose a self addressed stamped 6" by 9" envelope ($.50 postage) with your request.

13. IS IT PERMISSIBLE TO PERFORM COPYRIGHTED RELI-GIOUS WORKS IN CHURCH?

Yes. You may perform copyrighted religious works from legal editions in the course of services at places of worship or at religious assemblies. Legal editions do not result from unauthorized duplication of religious works: i.e., to purchase one copy of religious sheet music, then make 30 copies for the choir without permission and then perform it in a worship service is not legal or ethical.

14. CAN I MAKE AN ORIGINAL RECORDING OF A COPY-RIGHTED SONG?

Yes, but you must secure a recording license from the copyright owner, and pay, effective January 1, 1988, a royalty of 5 1/4 cents per song, per record, or tape manufactured. (This rate increases every two years.) *This includes copies of recordings or tapes of church services, concerts, musicals, or any programs that include copyrighted music.*

15. CAN I MAKE A RECORD OR TAPE USING A PRE-RE-CORDED INSTRUMENTAL ACCOMPANIMENT TRACK?

Yes, provided you have proper permission; and two different permissions are necessary in this situation. The first is from the copyright owner of the selection to be recorded (see question 13), and the second is from the producer/manufacturer of the accompaniment track. Fees are usually required for each permission.

16. IS IT PERMISSIBLE TO MAKE DUPLICATES OF THE TAPE THAT ACCOMPANIES A MUSICAL OR PRINTED WORK FOR "LEARNING" OR "REHEARSAL" PURPOSES?

NO, *it is illegal.* As good an idea as this is, and as helpful as it would be to teach the music to members of the choir, it is against the law without permission. Write or call the publisher of the music. They will usually work with you concerning your request.

17. IF I BUY A RECORD, IS IT PERMISSIBLE TO MAKE A COPY FOR A FRIEND?

Duplication of copyrighted materials is against the law when the purpose avoids a legal purchase.

18. WHAT ARE THE PENALTIES FOR MAKING UNAUTHO-RIZED COPIES OF COPYRIGHTED MUSIC?

Embarrassment is the first. Additionally, the law provides for the owners of a copyright to recover damages for unauthorized use of copyrighted music. These damages include the profits of the in-fringer and statutory damages ranging from not less than $250 to not more than $50, 000 per infringement. In addition, prison terms are provided for willful (i.e., you knew what you were doing was wrong!) and commercial infringement. Remember, churches, schools and not-for-profit organization can be infringers too!

19. WHAT ABOUT PHOTOCOPIERS WHO DON'T "GET CAUGHT"?

Frankly, we cannot imagine what kind of school, church or pro-fessional musician would derive satisfaction from doing something illegal. They force the price of legal editions higher. They risk embar-rassment from professional colleagues who understand the law. They risk fines and jail sentences if taken to court.

Plainly stated, ***the making of unauthorized copies of all copyrighted material is strictly illegal.*** However, all music pub-lishers desire to have their songs used in as many ways as possible; so in some cases, permission can be obtained. You must contact the copyright owner prior to use or duplication.

POSTLUDE

Information in this section is taken from a brochure produced by the Church Music Publishers Association and is issued by the follow-ing organizations:

American Choral Directors Association
American Guild of Organists
Association of Disciple Musicians

Choral Conductors Guild
Choristers Guild
Evangelical Lutheran Church
Fellowship In The Arts—United Church of Christ
Fellowship of American Baptist Musicians
Fellowship of United Methodists in Worship Music and   Other
Arts
Gospel Music Association
Hymn Society of America
Music Educators National Convention
Music Publishers Association
National Association of Church Musicians - Church of
    God
National Association of Pastoral Musicians
National Association of Schools of Music
National Church Music Fellowship
National Music Publishers Association
Presbyterian Association of Musicians
Retail Sheet Music Dealers Association
Southern Baptist Church Music Conference
Standing Commission of Church Music of the Episcopal
    Church

If you have further questions, please feel free to ask a publisher or direct your inquiries to the Church Music Publishers Association, P.O. Box 158992, Nashville TN 37215. CMPA and it's member publishers are always willing to help you with copyright questions. CMPA has installed a 24-hour-a-day "hotline" number to service church musicians and provide information. Call (615)791-0273.

RESOURCE MATERIALS

Choir By-Laws

Retreat Schedule

Sample Bulletins of Worship Services

BY-LAWS OF
THE CATHEDRAL CHOIR
First Presbyterian Church of Hollywood

Preamble

"Make a joyful noise unto the Lord, all ye lands. Serve the Lord with gladness; come before His presence with singing."
Psalm 100

We, as members of the Cathedral Choir, pray that our ministry of music might make hearts more receptive to the Lord, glorifying Him through the medium of fine, worshipful music; and that we may attain a position of spiritual and cultural leadership in the community.

We agree to devote our efforts to this end, that we may participate fully in the blessings that come with accomplishment.

We look to our Director for musical development and to our elected officers for leadership in spiritual and social growth.

We recognize the need to serve wherever needed for the welfare of the Choir and will subordinate our individual prominence to its rightful place in relation to the group.

ARTICLE I
Membership

To the end that the Choir may be constantly at its highest degree of effectiveness, the members shall be chosen annually on the basis of musical ability, cooperation, spirit and faithfulness of attendance and effort. Letters of invitation will be sent to reappointed and newly-appointed members each year during the summer hiatus.

New member orientation shall include a letter of welcome by the President accompanied by the current Membership Directory. In addition, during the first month of service, it shall be the responsibility of the Personnel Chairman, with the assistance of the appropriate Part Superintendent, to schedule a briefing prior to the new member's first Sunday. This briefing shall include a complete "walk-through" of the service. Folder and robe numbers will be assigned as soon as possible by the Personnel Chairman.

ARTICLE II
Attendance

Rehearsals are held from 7:30 to 10:00 P.M. every Thursday during the regular Choir season unless otherwise specified by the Director.

Members are expected to attend both Sunday morning services. They are to report robed and ready to sing at the appointed time.

Members are expected to attend all scheduled performances together with all associated rehearsals.

Any member failing to attend Thursday rehearsal will not sing on Sunday morning unless exception is granted by the Director.

ARTICLE III
Absences

Any absence from rehearsal or services MUST be reported in advance to Part Superintendent to facilitate seating.

Only absences caused by illness and similar emergencies will be considered excusable.

More than three unexcused absences will be brought to the attention of the Personnel Chairman and Director by the Part Superintendent for appropriate action.

In addition, two weeks of vacation will be allowed each member during each Choir season.

A leave of absence is entirely at the discretion of the Director. Return to the Choir will depend on current needs.

ARTICLE IV
Finance

Dues shall be assessed to each member every year. The amount to be charged shall be set by the Cabinet upon the recommendation of the Executive Committee.

Dues shall be payable no later than October 30 and shall be used for the purposes of current Choir expenses.

New members entering the Choir during the year shall be required to pay dues at the rate of one-tenth the annual dues per month for the remainder of the year, payable thirty days after attendance at the first rehearsal.

The Executive Committee will give approval before expenditures in excess of guidelines set in the annual budget.

Bank accounts shall be established from which to pay Choir expenses and all checks written shall be signed by any two of the following: President, Vice President, Treasurer.

ARTICLE V
Election of Officers

On the first Thursday in May, the President will announce the appointment of a Nominating Committee (see ARTICLE VII, Section B). A recommendation sheet will be distributed to the Choir members to solicit suggestions for officers.

On the third Thursday in May, the Nominating Committee will make its report and recommendations to the Choir. Further nominations from the floor will be accepted. In the event of additional nominations from the floor, a secret ballot will be taken. Otherwise, the Secretary will be instructed to cast a unanimous ballot for the Nominating Commmittee's choice.

Vacancies on the Cabinet will be filled by a vote of the remaining members of the Cabinet. Acting members may be appointed by the Executive Committee pending Cabinet action.

New officers shall assume their duties on July 1 of the year of election and shall terminate their duties as of June 30 of the following year.

ARTICLE VI
Officers and Management

The officers of the Choir shall be referred to collectively as the Cabinet. The Cabinet shall be the primary policy-making body, and shall consist of the following:

(1) President
(2) Vice President
(3) Secretary
(4) Treasurer
(5) Personnel

171

(6)   Social
(7)   Dinner Club
(8)   Librarians
(9)   Property
(10) Historian
(11) Publicity
(12) Chaplain
(13) Workshop
(14) Retreat
(15) Part Superintendent—Soprano
(16) Part Superintendent—Alto
(17) Part Superintendent—Tenor
(18) Part Superintendent—Bass

Each officer shall maintain records throughout the year as to the activities of the office and submit the same to the incoming officer in order to facilitate a smooth transition in carrying forward the Choir program. These records shall be cumulative and kept for a period of three years. Thereafter, the records shall be delivered to the Historian to be kept indefinitely until a decision is made by the Cabinet to destroy the same.

A.   **President.**

Qualifications:

1. One (1) year Hollywood Presbyterian Church membership.
2. Four (4) years Cathedral Choir membership.
3. Two (2) years Cabinet Service, one of which on the Executive Committee level.

Responsibilities:

The President shall be the chief executive officer of the Choir and shall, subject to the counsel of the Director, have general supervision and control of the business of the Choir. The President shall:

1. Preside at all meetings of the Cabinet and the Choir.
2. Be a member of all standing committees (see ARTICLE VII).
3. Call all meetings of the Cabinet.
4. Chair the Executive Committee.

5. Report the important business conducted at the Cabinet meetings to the Choir.

6. Appoint a Nominating Committee.

7. Represent or appoint a representative for the Choir at functions that require same.

8. Prepare a personal letter of welcome to all new members.

9. Interface with Session through the Music Committee and Choir members serving on Session.

10. Assume any other duties or exercise such power as may be prescribed to the President of any organization.

11. Act in an advisory capacity at all Cabinet meetings in the year subsequent to service.

12. Initiate correspondence in connection with expressions of appreciation for gifts or any other occasion requiring same.

13. Coordinate additional activities of the Choir, including, but not limited to concerts, recordings and tours, but excluding the Labor Day Workshop, Midyear Retreat and social events.

14. Appoint ad hoc committees as needed.

B. **Vice President.**

In the absence or disability of the President, the Vice President shall perform all duties of the President, and when so acting shall have all the powers of, and be subject to all the restrictions upon the President. Should the President for any reason not serve a complete term of office, the Vice President shall become President and an acting Vice President shall be appointed by the Executive Committee pending approval by the Cabinet as provided in ARTICLE V. In addition, the Vice President shall:

1. Plan and coordinate all receptions and luncheons in conjunction with the Music Committee.

2. Be a member of the Executive Committee.

3. Be responsible for the purchase and presentation of all gifts given at the Spring Banquet, including the presentation of a gavel to the out-going President and 25-year Cathedral Choir service awards.

4. Send flowers or plants to Choir members or family who are ill, and present wedding gifts or baby gifts where appropriate.

5. Serve as a contact between the Choir and Choir Mothers and Coffee Hostesses.

C. **Secretary.**

The Secretary shall:

1. Keep complete and accurate minutes of all Cabinet and Executive Committee meetings, these minutes to be reviewed and approved by the President before posting.

2. Provide copies of minutes to the Director and President.

3. Post a copy of the minutes of the Cabinet and Executive Committee meetings in a prominent place in the rehearsal room.

4. Be a member of the Executive Committee.

5. Keep an up-to-date copy of the By-Laws of the Choir.

6. Prepare all correspondence requested by the President.

7. Maintain an up-to-date alumni/friends file.

8. Prepare and mail invitations to special Choir events as directed by the Cabinet.

D. **Treasurer.**

The Treasurer shall:

1. Keep and maintain adequate and correct accounts of the financial transactions of the Choir; including receipts, disbursements and so on.

2. Deposit all monies received to the credit of the Choir with such depositories as may be designated from time to time by the Cabinet.

3. Be responsible for collecting all charges to be assessed for dinners and social events.

4. Be prepared to give reports at all Cabinet meetings as to the status of the treasury.

5. Prepare and submit to the Executive Committee a preliminary summary of the year's financial activities as of June 1 and a final report to be given to the successor Treasurer on July 1.

6. Collect the dues assessed to each member.

7. Be a member of the Executive Committee.

8. Pay all bills accruing to the Choir.

E. **Property.**

Qualifications: Attendance at no less than one (1) previous Workshop.

The Property Manager shall:

1. Care for and keep records of all materials and properties of the Choir with the exception of music.

2. Check with the Director thirty minutes prior to services as to the Director's stand and platform, and coordinate with the Personnel Chairman as to the necessity for additional chairs in the loft. If the Property Manager shall be absent from any rehearsal or performance, he shall designate a substitute and inform the Director whom he has so designated.

3. Prepare loft for specific performances (remove podium and facade and replacement thereof).

4. Report any major repairs necessary to the floors, seats, etc., to the Music Secretary.

5. Be responsible for arrangement of equipment at the request of the Director.

F. **Librarians.**

The Librarians shall:

1. Be in charge of all Choir music.

2. See that music requested by the Director is available to Choir members prior to and during each rehearsal.

3. Collect and refile all music after use or when it is no longer needed in the folder.

4. Prepare chalkboards with order of music for services.

5. Keep the selection of music currently being used in the Music Library rack.

6. Assign folder numbers to new members as directed by the Personnel Chairman.

7. Coordinate the transportation, arrangement, distributon and protection of all music and folders in connection with any special concerts.

There shall be an Assistant Librarian elected who shall work at the direction of, and shall assist in all the functions and duties of the Librarian.

G. **Social.**

The Social Chairman shall:

1. Appoint and preside over a committee (if needed) which will plan, arrange and take charge of the Christmas party, Spring Banquet and all other events to be scheduled.
2. Reserve Church meeting rooms and equipment for special events except Dinner Clubs.
3. Budget each social event to be self-supporting unless otherwise authorized by the Cabinet.

H. **Dinner Club.**

The Dinner Club Chairman shall be in charge of Dinner Clubs when scheduled, and if needed, appoint and preside over a committee to assist with reservations, decorations, program, etc.

I. **Personnel.**

The Personnel Chairman shall:

1. Confer with the Director and make up a seating chart, both for the sanctuary and rehearsal.
2. Verify absences and make up seating chart for all performances.
3. Arrange for nursery and/or child care for Choir children, if necessary, for any special rehearsal or performance.
4. Be a member of the Executive Committee.
5. Present the Choir Rules of Etiquette, as the same is from time to time amended, at the beginning of each new season, and comment thereon from time to time as needed.
6. Appoint and preside over a committee to update and change the Rules of Etiquette if necessary, and make any such changes available for inclusion in the Directory.

7. Be responsible for orientation of new members and inform Librarian of robe number.

8. Meet with the Choir Mothers and arrange for robe assignments for new members.

9. Submit a list of all new members to the Music Secretary so that the same can be distributed at the first Thursday evening rehearsal following the Labor Day Workshop.

J. **Part Superintendent.**

All Part Superintendents shall:

1. Keep accurate records of attendance on cards furnished by Music Secretary.

2. Give a report at rehearsals as to which members of the section are absent, and the reason therefor.

3. Assist in the orientation of all new members entering section during the year.

4. Collect new music for members reporting absences in advance to Part Superintendent and relay important announcements made at rehearsal to those reporting absent members.

K. **Chaplain.**

The Chaplain shall:

1. Offer prayer or arrange for a substitute to offer prayer at the beginning and ending of each rehearsal and at such other times as seem appropriate.

2. Visit all Choir members who are hospitalized, if possible.

L. **Historian.**

The Historian shall:

1. Collect and enter into the Choir Scrapbook all printed material and pictures available pertaining to or of special interest to the Choir or its activities.

2. Supervise the protection of previous year's scrapbooks, including arranging times for them to be displayed.

3. Maintain on the Church premises the records of officers over three years old, and advise the Cabinet as to when the same should be destroyed.

M. **Publicity.**

Qualificatons: Attendance at no less than one (1) previous Workshop.

The Publicity Chairman shall:

1. Publicize all Choir concerts and musical programs.
2. Prepare and distribute brochures for special events.
3. Prepare the "Downbeat" for distribution at the fall workshop as a preview of the new year.
4. Assist the Music Department in maintenance of the publicity mailing list.
5. Prepare an annual Directory of members to be distributed no later than the first October rehearsal. This Directory shall also contain the current By-Laws, Workshop duties and Rules of Etiquette.
6. Prepare an update of the Directory to be distributed in January as needed.

N. **Workshop**

The Workshop Chairman shall plan and coordinate the assignment of responsibilities for the Labor Day Workshop, including the necessary follow-up with the Cabinet members to see that duties are carried out.

O. **Retreat.**

The Retreat Chairman shall:

1. Assist the Workshop Chairman in the planning and coordination of the Labor Day Workshop.
2. Assume the office of Workshop Chairman the following year.
3. Be in charge of the Midyear Retreat.

ARTICLE VII
Committees

There shall be four standing committees, i.e., Executive, Nominating, Workshop Review, and Memorial Funds.

A. **Executive Committee.**

The Executive Committee shall be comprised of the President (Chairman), Vice President, Secretary, Treasurer and

Personnel Chairman. It shall be responsible for implementation of Choir Cabinet policy and shall be accountable to the Cabinet for its actions. The Committee's purposes shall be to:

1. Prepare a budget to be presented by the Treasurer at the first Cabinet meeting of each season.
2. Prepare a budget in concert with the Workshop Chairman to be used to determine charges for the Workshop in time for mailing the reservation sheet.
3. Assume the duties assigned in Article IV.
4. Implement fund-raising as authorized by the Cabinet.
5. Receive gifts to the Choir which do not qualify as memorial funds (as defined in Article VII D) and deposit same in the Choir treasury.
6. At the end of the year prepare budget recommendations for newly elected Executive Committee.

B. **Nominating Committee**

The Nominating Committee shall be appointed by the President and announced to the Choir on the first Thursday in May. The Committee shall consist of one member from each section, plus the President and the Director. A recommendation sheet will be distributed to the Choir members to solicit suggestions for officers. On the third Thursday in May, the Committee will make its report and recommendations to the Choir.

C. **Workshop Review Committee.**

There shall be a committee to review the mechanics of the last-past Workshop with a view toward alleviating any problems for the next year's Workshop. This Committee shall meet as soon as possible after the Labor Day Workshop and shall consist of at least the following: Workshop Chairman, Retreat Chairman, Director, President, Personnel Chairman, and Property Manager.

D. **Memorial Funds Board of Directors:**

The Memorial Funds Board of Directors shall receive and administer all memorial funds and shall be responsible for carrying out any specified purpose or the formation of programs for the use of those funds without a specified purpose delineated. Memorial funds shall be defined as gifts given in someone's name with or without a specified purpose delineated. The Board shall consist of three rotating Choir members and permanent Treasurer, Liaison Officer as might be needed to represent a specific fund, and Secretary plus the current Choir President and Choir Treasurer. One rotating choir member shall be elected each year during the annual election of officers (see Article V) and shall serve three years. The ranking rotating member (the member in the third term year) shall be Chairman. The Board Treasurer, Liaison Officer, and Secretary shall be chosen by the current Memorial Funds Board of Directors whenever a vacancy occurs. The Board Treasurer shall submit a quarterly report of the status of each fund to the Board, and a yearly report shall be submitted to the June Cabinet meeting, a copy of these reports to be kept in the Music Office. The Board Secretary shall keep an up-to-date record of all business of the Memorial Funds Board of Directors.

E. **Etiquette.**

The Personnel Chairman shall make a recommendation to the Cabinet when the Rules of Etiquette need to be updated, and if approved by the Cabinet, shall appoint a Committee to do so. Said Committee shall make its recommendations to the Cabinet.

F. **Social.**

The Social Chairman shall have the authority to appoint a Committee to assist in the organization and preparation of all social events, if deemed necessary in the sole and absolute discretion of the Social Chairman.

G. **Dinner Club.**

The Dinner Club Chairman shall have the authority to appoint a Committee to assist in the organization and preparation of all Dinner Clubs, if it is deemed necessary in the sole and absolute discretion of the Dinner Club Chairman.

ARTICLE VIII
Miscellaneous
A. **Amendments to the By-Laws.**

These By-Laws may be repealed or amended, or new By-Laws may be adopted at any Cabinet meeting. Initiation of repeals or amendments may be made by any Choir member. The amendments as adopted by the Cabinet shall be presented to a business meeting of the Choir and voted upon by the members present, a two-thirds vote being necessary for ratification. Whenever an amendment or new By-Law is adopted, it shall be copied in the original By-Laws which are to be kept by the Secretary in the Book of Minutes of the Choir.

The By-Laws, as amended, shall be reprinted in the Directory each year in order to be a handy reference for the conduct of the Choir business.

B. **Workshop Duties and Procedures.**

The Workshop duties and procedures, as updated each year by the Workshop Review Committee, shall be printed in the Directory each year in order to be a handy reference for the conduct of the Workshop.

C. **Rules of Etiquette**

The current Rules of Etiquette shall be printed in the Directory each year in order to be a handy reference.

CATHEDRAL CHOIR ETIQUETTE

The following rules of Choir Etiquette are designed that we might glorify our Lord more effectively in a simple and digni-fied manner, discouraging movement which draws the atten-tion of worshippers to the individual Choir member and away from the purpose of the worship service.

1. Report to your Part Superintendent if unable to attend rehearsal or service at the *earliest possible time.* If you cannot contact your own Superintendent, contact the Per-sonnel Chairman or any other Part Superintendent. Planned absences (i.e., vacations, business trips, etc.) should be reported to the Director at the *earliest possible time.*

2. Sunday morning, all should be robed and seated, music in hand, at 8:45 in the rehearsal room. NO tea or coffee at seats.

3. Women should not wear earrings (exception: pierced ears, non-shiny posts only), necklaces, dangling bracelets, ribbons, head bands or barrettes (exception: those that are same color as hair and not seen from the front).

4. For processionals, men should wear dark trousers; women should not wear slacks; both should wear dark shoes and neither should have collars showing. If necessary, shirts or blouses should be removed.

5. Carry folder in left hand, using a flexed position.

6. In the loft, be alert to Director's signal system: 4 fingers, back row; 3 fingers, next to back row; 2 fingers, quartet row; 1 finger, front row. Be alert to stand and sit in unison with Director.

7. When you are the first person in each row to enter the loft, wait at the door for a downbeat signal from the Director before entering. Do **not** look at the door on the other side.

8. Do not show any recognition of family or friends in the congregation.

9. Avoid excessive arm movements. The cotta robe combination creates a considerable distraction by crossing arms, reaching into pockets, fanning, etc. Hold music as evenly as possible with others in row and be alert to standing position so that others can see the Director also.

10. Use good posture in sitting and standing; rise with one foot slightly ahead of the other to assist in balance and vertical rising. When sitting, wait for those on ends to turn or move into places. Knees should be kept together at all times when seated.

11. The folder is to be kept on lap at all times when not singing; use the folder as announced by the Director.

12. Arise with Director for hymns. The first and last verses should be sung in unison and the middle verses in four-part harmony unless otherwise directed. Hymns for the day should have been clipped by page number before coming into the loft. After hymn, be seated with Director.

13. As we rise to sing anthem, open the folder. Hold the folder with the left hand and use the right hand to turn pages. As we sit after anthem, close folder quietly onto lap.

14. During any prayer, heads should be bowed and backs vertical, touching the back of the pew, rather than in a hunched position. Be alert for musical responses.

15. After closing response, stand on signal with folder and hymnal in left arm position and wait for Director's signal.

16. You are in the loft to WORSHIP, not TALK. Remain silent and maintain a reverent attitude.

ANNUAL WORKSHOP
Responsibilities of Cabinet Officers

A. **Director**

1. Consult with Workshop Chairman re: guest Chaplain selected by Cabinet.

2. Prepare letter of invitation to members for the coming year and transmit to the Music Secretary and Workshop Chairman by June 10.

B. **Music Office Secretary**

1. Assist Workshop Chairman with official correspondence.

2. Prepare, edit and address invitational mailing and work with Publicity Chairman to distribute prior to close of current Choir year. The complete package should include:

   a. Invitational letter from Director.
   b. Welcome letter from the President.
   c. Reservation form.
   e. Map of campus.
   f. *Downbeat* information request form.

C. **Workshop Chairman**

1. Have overall responsibility for Workshop, including planning and coordination.

2. Send letter to Academy in April securing facilities and expenses. Following receipt of reply, contact President and arrange for Executive Committee to prepare a proposed budget.

3. After discussion with the Director and Cabinet, select and invite guest Chaplain in March or April.

4. Review the "Annual Workshop Report" prepared following the previous Workshop and distribute to new Cabinet at June meeting of old and new Cabinets.

5. Coordinate with Music Secretary in the preparation of the invitational mailing materials. See B above.

6. Coordinate with the President to schedule summer meeting of the Cabinet to finalize basic plans for the Workshop. It should be held shortly after the deadline date for receiving reservations. Finalize official schedule of events for typing by Music Secretary. The usual number of copies printed is 200.

7. If it is considered necessary, arrange for a trip to Academy during the summer by key Workshop personnel to meet with and coordinate the conduct of the Workshop with the supervisory personnel at the Academy. Suggested attendees include: Workshop, Retreat, Property and Personnel Chairmen and the Treasurer.

8. Secure lifeguard services. They shall be paid what the Academy suggests is fair. However, overtime should not be paid to some while others earn the minimum salary and work fewer hours. Make sure the Academy understands this stipulation. Schedules for lifeguard services must be sent in August letter to the Academy.

9. As needed, make necessary arrangements for a program of planned games and recreation for children in the age groups 4-6 and 7-9 years. (Personnel Chairman will advise number requesting planned activities after reservations are tabulated.) It is suggested that separate activities be planned for each age group during the longer morning rehearsals only. Adequate adult supervision must be secured ahead of time for each activity group. Be sure that the requested books, records, record players, games, puzzles, athletic equipment, etc., will be available.

10. Arrange for photographer for picture of group and new Cabinet. Find out when he will arrive, number in party and how many meals they will have. Give information to Personnel Chairman and Treasurer.

11. Arrange for preparation and editing of the list of extracurricular activities to be distributed at registration.

Coordinate list of items with Social, Personnel and Property Chairmen. Check availability of all equipment needs during the preliminary trip to the Academy.

12. Advise Academy, no later than one week prior to Workshop, of anticipated number of attendees, planned activity schedule and a confirmation of equipment needs.

13. Determine who can arrive at the Academy early on Friday to take care of early check-ins and handle any other matters that may require attention. Have copy of attendees and their room assignments available on *Friday morning* for early arrivees at the Academy and post on Commandant's Office door or post a person there with the information. This will enable early arrivals to "move in" on arrival. It is also desirable to check all rooms prior to arrival of attendees for plumbing problems, doors needing to be unlocked, etc.

14. Make arrangements to obtain necessary keys. Those needed in past Workshops include: 1) organ; 2) piano; 3) room 112; 4) band room; 5) pass or master; 6) recreation hall; 7) kitchen; 8) safe (Treasurer); 9) tennis courts; 10) Commandants Office; 11) beach; 12) Chapel and restrooms; and 13) master for sleeping rooms (in case someone locks himself out).

15. Determine when Academy personnel will be leaving the campus for the weekend, when the duty officer and maintenance man will be on campus, and how to reach Academy after hours. Normal number is 619/729-2385.

16. Coordinate with the Academy to establish the amount of advance payment required (usually $2,000). Make certain the Treasurer comes prepared to make the advance payment and that payment is made upon arrival.

17. During the summer visit, inquire or check if rehearsal room piano is in tune. If not, endeavor to get it tuned before Workshop starts.

18. Post schedule of activities on bulletin board by cafeteria on Friday.

19. At the first rehearsal, announce that the Treasurer must be advised of all expected guests for meals, particularly Sunday lunch. This will insure that enough food will be

prepared. Advise the Chef immediately if there are significant changes from the numbers given in the advance letter.

20. At the close of the Workshop, follow up with the Treasurer on payments to personnel and with the Property Chairman on the cleaning of the campus.

21. In late September, follow up with the Treasurer to insure that accounting is done and final payment made to Academy.

22. Prepare and distribute a questionnaire to obtain suggestions for improving the next Workshop. Also request officers to submit written reports. Follow up to make sure every officer complies.

23. Ask President to call a Cabinet meeting in early October to review Workshop.

24. Using the questionnaires, officers' reports and notes from the follow-up meeting, with the Retreat Chairman, write the "Annual Workshop Report" for the Workshop just completed. This becomes the working papers for the next Workshop and must be up to date and complete.

D. Retreat Chairman

1. Provide assistance to Workshop Chairman as requested prior to, during and after the Workshop.

2. Carefully observe the planning and conduct of the Workshop so as to be as well-informed as possible to take over the responsibilities of Workshop Chairman the following year.

3. Help Personnel Chairman in assembling packets.

4. Arrange for name tags. Pin-on or clip-on badges are recommended for Choir members and adhesive tags for guests. Wrist bands shall be provided for everyone to facilitate identification of paid attendees at the cafeteria.

5. Coordinate incoming telephone calls for Choir personnel with Academy personnel. If Cabinet directs, make arrangements for an answering service and advise Workshop Chairman of the number for inclusion in Workshop invitational mailing.

6. Work out schedule with Workshop Chairman for locking and unlocking various areas. Lock Recreation Hall during all major events such as Chapel services and the evening programs. Make sure all buildings of general use are secured after taps. Work closely with Property Chairman and Social Chairmen on the use of keys.

7. Meet with Workshop Chairman to prepare the "Annual Workshop Report" regarding the completed Workshop.

E. **President**

1. Follow up with Workshop Chairman to see that all assigned duties are being done in a timely manner.

2. Schedule Cabinet meetings as required for proper planning of Workshop. Note that planning should be initiated shortly after new officers are elected. Cabinet meetings should include a meeting of the outgoing and incoming Cabinets wherein outgoing officers should convey pertinent information to the incoming officers which will be of value in the conduct of the upcoming Workshop.

3. Prepare a letter to be included as part of the invitational package to all Choir members. Transmit to the Music Secretary and Workshop Chairman by June 10.

4. Contact new members to personally welcome them into the Choir family, i.e., perhaps by a letter of greeting and welcome.

5. Convene Executive Committee following the April contact with the Academy and supervise the preparation of a proposed budget for the Workshop.

F. **Vice President**

1. Plan, organize and be responsible for Friday evening refreshments, including coordination of equipment needs with the Property Manager and Workshop Chairman.

2. Arrange for marshmallows, sticks, etc. for bonfire. Academy will provide wood. Ask Property Chairman to make certain that firewood, etc. is requested.

3. Purchase and present gifts to Chef and assistant.

G. **Treasurer**

1. Receive all registration and dues from Personnel Chairman, together with list of Workshop attendees.

2. Arrive no later than 6 p.m. on Friday. At registration, collect cash and checks from members and guests who have not prepaid. Also collect from part-time attendees as they arrive.

3. On Monday morning of Workshop weekend, make disbursements to Academy for services by their personnel.

4. Make disbursements to Social Chairman and Vice President for their expenses, either at the Workshop or later.

5. Request Music Secretary to get check from the Church representing its contribution toward Workshop expenses. Deposit check in the Choir account.

6. Contact Church Business Manager to confirm that Choir is still covered by the normal group insurance which we have used in the past.

7. After registration is essentially over, summarize attendance and compare with number previously given to the Academy by the Workshop Chairman. If there is significant difference, discuss with Workshop Chairman immediately so that the Chef may be notified.

8. Prepare meal tickets for guests and establish a mealtime cashier and ticket taker. Supply meal tickets in advance to part-timers in their registration packet.

9. Immediately after return from Workshop, prepare final summary of attendance and meal charges. Cross-check numbers with final reservations for differences. Send summary and check to Academy.

10. Prepare final income and expense report and submit to the Cabinet.

11. With the Workshop Chairman and Executive Committee, prepare a projected budget of revenues and expenditures for the next year. Last year's final budget report should be available for presentation, along with the Executive Committee's proposed Workshop budget, at the June Cabinet meeting. The final budget should be presented and approved at the August Cabinet meeting.

H. Personnel Chairman

1. With the Director and Cabinet, prepare a list of guests to be invited and coordinate with the Music Secretary the issuance of invitations. Usual invitees include the coffee servers, Choir Mothers, active Elders, Church executive staff and any others designated by the Cabinet.

2. Receive and tabulate all reservations. Forward checks to Treasurer. Reservation deadline will be determined at the Cabinet meeting. Usually 3 to 4 weeks are allowed between distribution and cutoff.

3. Report reservations tabulations to Workshop Chairman immediately after deadline. The breakdown should identify the number of full-time attendees: age 12 and over; age 9-11; age 4-8; and those 3 and under. For part-time attendees, specify details on meals and lodging.

4. Engage babysitter to care for children through 3 years. They will be retained for rehearsal hours and Chapel services only and are usually provided for members only, whether one or both parents are Choir members. Payment usually includes meals and lodging and a small amount of cash to be determined by the Cabinet. (Babysitters may be engaged for "bed checks" during Saturday and Sunday evening programs for an additional $1.00 per family. Arrangements are to be made directly between babysitters and family.)

5. Prepare an official listing of all Workshop attendees not later than ten days prior to the Workshop, identifying all members and guests. Forward as soon as possible to Director, Assistant Workshop Chairman, Music Secretary and Librarian.

6. Check with Workshop Chairman approximately five days before Workshop for any variations or restrictions on room availability. Make room assignments for attendees and prepare master plan for entire campus. Also prepare individual map for each registration packet. OPTIONAL: Set date for and attend the summer visit to Academy.

7. Notify each Part Superintendents of the names, etc. of all new members in their sections.

8. Turn over reservation forms to Treasurer prior to Friday evening check-in.

9. Contact Property Manager concerning anyone needing a ride to the Workshop.

10. Prepare registration packets for each family or individual containing Schedule, campus map with housing assignment, name tag(s), wrist band(s).

11. Establish registration center at Workshop and provide staff therefor from 6 to 11 p.m. on Friday.

12. Follow up on late arrivals. Post campus map on Commandant's Office door or wherever check-in is to take place, so that late arrivals can visibly see where their rooms are.

13. Obtain seating chart from Director; make name tags on masking tape and place on rehearsal room chairs. Forward seating chart to Historian for rehearsal room set-up.

14. Secure green enrollment cards from Music Secretary for the Choir to fill out and return to their part superintendents.

15. Enlist Part Superintendents to assist whenever necessary.

I. **Chaplain**

1. Arrange and have general responsibility for all worship services, including the Saturday convocation, Sunday morning worship, Sunday evening vespers and Monday dedication (including arrangements for Communion).

2. Coordinate all worship service planning with guest Chaplain selected by Cabinet.

3. Plan Sunday School classes and secure teachers.

4. Assign responsibility for prayer at meals and rehearsals.

5. Appoint director for new or firsttime Workshop attendees (Choir members) to form Choir to sing at Sunday morning worship.

6. Typical programming for services:

   Saturday: Two hymns, prayer, scripture and message.

   Sunday: Two hymns, prayer, anthem, scripture and message.

   Make sure organist knows he is expected to play for these services, including appropriate preludes and postludes, etc.

8. After Workshop, send letter of appreciation to guest Chaplain.

J. Property Manager

1. Obtain from Personnel Chairman names of those needing rides and match with those who can provide rides.
2. Review with Workshop Chairman the list of properties the Academy provides.
3. Ask Choir members to provide the following:
   a. Fans
   b. Marshmallow forks for Friday night bonfire (Sprouses).
   c. Large ice chest to store ice daily for punch during breaks and for Director's water.
   d. Plunger for emergencies in ladies' restrooms.
   e. Lighter fluid, a pile of newspapers, and gloves, if desired, to start bonfire.
   f. Extra coffee urn as backup. See Dinner Club Chairman.
4. Arrange for building of bonfire for Friday night.
5. Secure a sound system. In the Chapel, the mike and amp are built into the pulpit. The switch is under pulpit.
6. Help secure movie projector, if needed.
7. Check on reveille arrangements with Paul Kilian and/or Richard Mancini.
8. Band room:
   a. Arrange chairs for first rehearsal (enlist Part Superintendents to assist whenever needed).
   b. Place fans strategically around room.
   c. Cover windows at rear with paper so afternoon sun is kept out. Windows may remain open a crack.
   d. Sweep and clean up, if needed.
   e. Place podium, music stand, and chalkboard.
9. Set up two long tables parallel to the bleachers in the corner of the gym nearest the gym "kitchen" for snacks. Make sure the floor underneath is covered with plastic, protecting the floor. Cover the top of the table with the same paper used to cover band windows.

10. Check to see if firewood is on beach. Be present at the lighting of the fire at 7:45 p.m. or so, and check area for safety. (If lots of kids, consider assigning an adult for supervision.)

11. Post the warning signs for the ladies' restrooms, one in each stall (approx. 25).

12. Get plastic pitcher and glass for Director from the kitchen staff.

13. Make sure refrigerator in Rec Hall is on by 6 p.m. on Friday and off by 1 p.m. on Monday.

14. Check sports equipment and make sure it's returned to Commandant's Office at end of retreat.

15. Each morning after breakfast, fill ice chest with ice from kitchen.

16. On Sunday, go to maintenance quarters and remind them that cleaning supplies will be needed on Monday. Request 2 mops, 4 cans of cleanser and several rags or paper towels.

17. On Monday assemble cleaning crews from new members, recruiting old members, if necessary. You will need 6 - 8 people. The bathrooms are to be swept and mopped, the sinks cleaned. Straighten the public meeting places, including the Commandant's office. Make certain nothing is left behind. Check with Maintenance Manager before leaving to see if everything the choir has done meets with his satisfaction.

K. Social Chairman

1. Arrange and have complete responsibility for Saturday and Sunday night's programs and refreshments. Form a committee to assist, including, but not limited to Part Superintendents, Historian and Dinner Club Chairman.

2. Submit list of equipment needs to Property Manager after June Cabinet meeting.

3. Enlist Part Superintendents to assist whenever necessary.

L. Librarians

1. Coordinate and be responsible for transporting, distributing, collecting and returning all music to be used at the Workshop, as requested by the Director.

M. Dinner Club Chairman

1. Assist Vice President with Friday night refreshments.

2. Assist Social Chairman with Saturday and Sunday evening refreshments.

3. Be responsible for all rehearsal coffee breaks, including securing assistance and specifying equipment needed through Property Manager.

N. Publicity Chairman

1. Arrange for publication of *Downbeat* for distribution at Workshop registration. This official Choir paper should include biographical material on new members, notes about summer activities, other noteworthy points relative to special church programs, Workshop highlights, etc. Approximately 150 copies should be printed.

O. Part Superintendents

1. The Personnel Chairman will provide the names, etc., of all new members of each section. Contact them well in advance of the Workshop to answer any questions and to help familiarize them with Choir rules and regulations. Offer assistance where needed and arrange for a buddy to personally assist in their first Workshop experience.

2. Personally welcome and assist all new members at the Workshop and make sure they have help getting into the "swing" of things relative to rehearsals, music folders, dining hall location, Workshop routines, etc.

3. Obtain background information on each new section member for use in personally introducing new member to Choir at an early Workshop rehearsal (before the first Coffee Break).

4. Have each Choir member complete a green enrollment card (provided by Music Secretary) and return completed cards to her.

5. Assist Personnel Chairman as requested.

6. Assist Social Chairman as requested.

7. Assist Property Manager as requested.

8. Assist any other Cabinet Officer whenever needed.

9. Report to Property Manager to organize final clean up.

P. Secretary

1. Work with Personnel Chairman to prepare names for rehearsal charts.
2. Assist Treasurer at registration.

THE 40TH ANNUAL
CATHEDRAL CHOIR WORKSHOP 1988
SCHEDULE OF EVENTS

FRIDAY, Sept. 2

6:00 p.m.	Registration *(check bulletin board for Dinner Dates?)*
8:00 p.m.	Bonfire and Social Time *(Oooh!!! Gusssshyyyyy!)*
11:00 p.m.	Registration Closes

SATURDAY, Sept. 3

7:30 a.m.	Reveille *(or a generic equivalent)*	12:30 p.m.	Lunch
8:00	Breakfast	4:30 p.m.	REHEARSAL No. 2
8:30	Free Time	6:30 p.m.	Dinner
8:45	Convocation (Chapel)	7:30 p.m.	Family "G" rated entertainment
	(Everybody Please!)	11:00 p.m.	Taps
9:20	REHEARSAL No. 1 (Band Room)		
	(Could never understand why a choir would rehearse in a band room)		

SUNDAY, Sept. 4

7:30 a.m.	Reveille	12:30 p.m.	Lunch
	(Sometimes it's really hard to tell!)	4:30 p.m.	REHEARSAL No. 4
8:00	Breakfast	6:30 p.m.	Dinner
8:45	Chapel	7:15 p.m.	Vespers (in Chapel) "Messiah"
9:30	REHEARSAL No. 3	8:30 p.m.	Showtime, rating unknown
12:05 p.m.	Cabinet picture (Dining Hall)	11:00 p.m.	Taps
	(This happens fast!)		
12:15	Group picture (Dining Hall)		
	(This happens even faster!!!)		

MONDAY, Sept. 5

7:30 a.m.	Reveille	12:30 p.m.	Lunch
	(You should have been there! We weren't)	1:00 p.m.	CLEAN UP TIME
8:00	Breakfast		First-timers and returnees, *"Beginning, Ground Level Course for Future Hotel Managers."*
8:45-10:15	REHEARSAL No. 5		
10:30-12:00	REHEARSAL No. 5 (Cont'd)		
	— open Communion		

NOTE: ALL ROOMS MUST BE LEFT IN SAME CONDITION AS UPON ARRIVAL, including **putting beds back together** (if taken apart). All damage is the personal responsibility of resident.

EXTRA-CURRICULAR ACTIVITIES

CATHEDRAL KIDS: (5-14)

Meet during rehearsals for crafts, games, music, devotions, and fun in Room 101 at southwest corner of Administration Blvd. (Gym)

CHAPEL SERVICES:

DICK DRUARY, Guest Chaplain — will speak at Convocation Services, Sunday AM Chapel and Vespers. Sunday school for those under 10 in Library.

BEACH AND SWIMMING POOL SCHEDULE:

	Beach	**Pool**
Beach Duty	Sat. 10:30 - 12:15 p.m.	Closed
2 Lifeguards	1:15 - 6:00 p.m.	1:15 - 4:15 p.m.
Pool Duty	Sun. 10:30 - 12:15 p.m.	Closed
1 Lifeguard	1:15 - 6:00 p.m.	1:15 - 4:15 p.m.
	Mon. 10:30 - 12:15 p.m.	Closed

THE BEACH WILL BE CLOSED WHEN THE LIFEGUARD SOUNDS SIREN AND GOES OFF DUTY!!! NO unattended children please!

Keeper of the keys this weekend is Kenneth Hart. Beach is off limits when gate is locked. Access available through public venues.

OTHER SPORTS:

> Tennis courts are available — bring your own equipment
> Volleyball on sand or grass
> Basketball
> Table Tennis
> Golfing in the area — check with Richard Mancini or John Bellish
> Athletic Field across Carlsbad Blvd. available for sports **IF NOT BEING USED BY CADETS.**

RECREATION HALL

> Snack Bar will be open from 1:30 - 5:00 p.m. Saturday and Sunday
> Table tennis
> Video games

First Presbyterian Church of Hollywood

1760 North Gower Street   Hollywood, California 90028
Lloyd John Ogilvie, Senior Pastor   Phone: (213) 463-7161 Valley: (818) 787-4651

MORNING WORSHIP   9:30 & 11:00 a.m.   JANUARY 3, 1988

*Congregation will stand.   * * *Ushers will seat delayed worshipers.

As a courtesy to other worshipers, please use the rear doors if you must leave before the service is over.

Hearing devices may be checked out from the Narthex prior to each service.
Please return them at the conclusion of the service.

Celebration of Worship

The Lord of New Beginnings

New Praise

9:25 and 10:55 Congregational Sung Preparation:

> He is Lord, He is Lord,
> He is risen from the dead and He is Lord,
> Every knee shall bow, every tongue confess
> That Jesus Christ is Lord.

Organ Prelude	*Fairest Lord Jesus* Kimo Smith, Organist	arr. David N. Johnson
Choral Adoration	*How Excellent is Thy Name, O Lord* Cathedral Choir/Dr. Fred Bock, Director	Melodie and Dick Tunney
Prayer of Adoration	9:30 Ralph Osborne	11:00 Jack Loo
***Hymn of Adoration No. 370**	*O God Our Help in Ages Past* (Stanza 3 unaccompanied)	ST. ANNE

* * *

New Life

Choral Call to Prayer	*I Need Jesus* Cathedral Choir	Charles H. Gabriel
Reponsive Reading	9:30 Dick Druary	11:00 Scott Erdman

Pastor: We say with Paul, "For I know whom I have believed and am persuaded that He is able to keep what I have committed to Him."
           (II Timothy 1:12)

Men: **All that we have and are is a gift from the Lord. Let us adore Him!**

Women: **He is Lord of the future. Let us trust Him!**

Pastor: There is no limit to what the Lord is able to do when we leave the results to Him. We adore Him when we lay our lives before Him in complete surrender.

All: **Lord, we adore You. Here are our minds, think through them; here are our emotions, love through them; here are our bodies, fill us with Your healing and shine through them. This is our prayer as we sing together:**

> **Father, I adore You, Lay my life before You,
> How I love You.**
>
> **Jesus, I adore You, Lay my life before You,
> How I love You.**
>
> **Spirit, I adore You, Lay my life before You,
> How I love You.**

Pastoral Prayer

Disciples' Prayer

* * *

Anthem   *Put on the Whole Armor of God*   John Ness Beck
                                              Cathedral Choir

Put on the full armor of God that you may be able to stand firm, having put on the breastplate of righteousness, and having shod your feet with the Gospel of peace, taking up the shield of faith, and the helmet of salvation, and the sword of the Spirit, which is the Word of God. Peace be to you, my brethren, and love with faith from God the Father and the Lord Jesus Christ. Grace be with all those who love our Lord Jesus Christ with a love incorruptible! Soldiers of Christ arise, and put your armor on, strong in the strength which God supplies through His eternal Son; strong in the Lord of Hosts, and in His mighty power, who in the strength of Jesus trusts, is more than conqueror. Amen. (Based on Ephesians 6:10-24; hymn text by Charles Wesley, 1707-1788)

New Joy

Sharing of the Joy

Tithes and Offerings

Offertory   *This Is the Time I Must Sing*   William J. Gaither
                                         Janet Payne, Soprano

*Doxology   OLD HUNDREDTH

*Prayer of Thanksgiving   9:30 Robert Loos   11:00 Robert Thompson

*Hymn No. 456   *My Jesus, I Love Thee*   GORDON
                                          Stanzas 1 and 2

New Hope

Reading of the Word of God   Ephesians 6:13-17

Prayer from the Word

Vision from The Word   Lloyd John Ogilvie

            Title: **Hopeful Thinking**

            Text: *Putting on the breastplate of faith and love, and as a helmet the hope of salvation.*   I Thessalonians 5:8

New Vision

Prayer of Dedication

Invitation

During and after the Hymn of Dedication, the Elders will be in the front of the Sanctuary to pray with and for you. Those who wish to receive Christ as Lord and Savior, those who desire prayer for spiritual, emotional and physical needs, those who need to commit their challenges and opportunities to the Lord for His guidance and intervening power, and those who are concerned about others are encouraged to come forward to kneel and pray.

*Hymn of Dedication No. 650   *I'd Rather Have Jesus*   SHEA

*Benediction

The congregation is requested to exit through the narthex rather than the doors at the front of the Sanctuary to facilitate the prayer ministry of the Elders at the steps of the chancel.

Playing of the Harold M. Ruddick Carillon

First Presbyterian Church of Hollywood

1760 North Gower Street
Lloyd John Ogilvie, Senior Pastor

Hollywood, California 90028
Phone: (213) 463-7161 Valley: (818) 787-4651

MORNING WORSHIP   9:30 & 11:00 a.m.   OCTOBER 4, 1987

*Congregation will stand.   * * *Ushers will seat delayed worshipers.

As a courtesy to other worshipers, please use the rear doors if you must leave before the service is over.

Hearing devices may be checked out from the Narthex prior to each service.
Please return them at the conclusion of the service.

Celebration of Worship
WORLD WIDE COMMUNION
Adoration

9:25 and 10:55   Silent Prayer and Preparation

Choral Preparation   *Holy Is the Lord*   Franz Schubert
Cathedral Choir/Dr. Fred Bock, Director

Responsive Reading   Jack Loo

Pastor: Holy, Holy, Holy, Holy is the Lord.

People: You are the Lord, we acclaim You.

Pastor: You are the eternal Father: all creation worships You.

**People: To You all angels, all the powers of heaven,
Cherubim and Seraphim, sing in endless praise:**

Women: Holy, Holy, Holy, Lord God of Hosts.

Pastor: Heaven and earth are full of Your glory.

Men: Glory be to You, O Lord most high.

Balcony only: Holy, Holy, Holy, Lord God of Hosts.

Pastor: Sanctus, Sanctus, Sanctus, Dominus Deus Sabaoth.

All: Holy, Holy, Holy, Lord God of Hosts.

Choral Adoration   *Sanctus* (from *Requiem*)   Maurice Duruflé

Sanctus, sanctus, sanctus,   Holy, holy, holy,
dominus Deus Sabaoth,   Lord God of hosts,
pleni sunt coeli et   Heaven and earth are full of
terra gloria tua.   Your glory.
Hosanna in excelsis,   Glory be to You, O Lord
                                            most high,
Benedictus qui venit in   Blessed is He, who comes
nomine Domini.   in the name of the Lord.

Invocation and Invitation to the Lord's Table
9:30 Dick Druary   11:00 Scott Erdman

*Hymn Of Praise No. 565   *A Hymn of Joy We Sing*   SCHUMANN

*Apostles' Creed No. 137

* * *

Confession

Choral Call to Prayer   *Fill Me Now*   John Sweney
                                  Cathedral Choir

Prayer of Confession   9:30 Ralph Osborne   11:00 Herbert Downie

Assurance of Pardon

Congregational Sung Response:

   Spirit of the Living God, fall afresh on me;
   Spirit of the Living God, fall afresh on me.
   Melt me, mold me, fill me, use me.
   Spirit of the Living God, fall afresh on me.

* * *

Thanksgiving

Tithes and Offerings

Offertory Anthem   *When I Survey the Wondrous Cross*   arr. Gilbert Martin
                                  Cathedral Choir

Prayer of Thanksgiving

Hope

Reading of God's Word   John 17:13-21

Communion Meditation   **FOREVER A FRIEND**   Jack Loo

Congregational Sung Response   *He Is Lord*   TRADITIONAL

Communion

Communion Prayer

Words of Institution

Distribution of the Means of Grace

Dedication

Congregational Sung Response:

      1. Alleluia!   4. I will praise Him.
      2. He's my Savior.   *5. I will serve Him!
      3. He is worthy.

Benediction

Choral Response   *Alleluia, Amen*   Eugene Butler

Organ Postlude   *Toccata* from *Symphony No. 5*   Charles Marie Widor
                          Kimo Smith, Organist

The Elders will be in the Reception Room to pray with and for you after the service.

First Presbyterian Church of Hollywood

1760 North Gower Street
Lloyd John Ogilvie, Senior Pastor

Hollywood, California 90028
Phone: (213) 463-7161 Valley: (818) 787-4651

MORNING WORSHIP   9:30 & 11:00 a.m.   MARCH 13, 1988

*Congregation will stand.   * * *Ushers will seat delayed worshipers.

As a courtesy to other worshipers, please use the rear doors if you must leave before the service is over.

Hearing devices may be checked out from the Narthex prior to each service.
Please return them at the conclusion of the service.

Fourth Sunday In Lent

CELEBRATION OF WORSHIP

Praise In The Spirit

Congregational Preparation: Doris Akers

> There's a sweet, sweet Spirit in this place, And I know that it's the Spirit of the Lord;
> There are sweet expressions on each face, And I know they feel the presence of the Lord.
> Sweet Holy Spirit, Sweet heavenly Dove, Stay right here with us,
> Filling us with Your love. And for these blessings we lift our hearts in praise;
> Without a doubt we'll know that we have been revived, When we shall leave this place.

© Manna Music Co. Used by permission.

9:25 and 10:55   Silent Prayer and Meditation

Organ Prelude   *Holy Spirit, Light Divine*   arr. Richard Purvis
Kimo Smith, Organist

Choral Adoration   *Alleluia, All Glory Be to God!*   Gordon Young
Cathedral Choir/Dr. Fred Bock, Director

*Confession of Our Faith: Apostles' Creed

I believe in God the Father Almighty, Maker of heaven and earth,

And in Jesus Christ His only Son our Lord; who was conceived by the Holy Spirit, born of the Virgin Mary, suffered under Pontius Pilate, was crucified, dead, and buried; He descended into hell; the third day He rose again from the dead; He ascended into Heaven, and sits on the right hand of God the Father Almighty; from there He shall come to judge the quick and the dead.

I believe in the Holy Spirit; the holy catholic Church; the communion of saints; the forgiveness of sins; the resurrection of the body; and the life everlasting.   Amen.

*Hymn of Praise No. 341   *Come, Thou Almighty King*   ITALIAN HYMN

Anthem from the Children   *Like As A Father*   Luigi Cherubini
Carol Choir/Gloria Kilian, Director   arr. Lovelace
Leslie Andersen, Violinist; Daniel Bondurant, Cellist; Philip Young, Pianist

* * *

Power In The Spirit

Choral Call to Prayer   *Fill Me Now*   John R. Sweney
Cathedral Choir

Prayer of Confession

Congregational Sung Response:

Come, Holy Spirit, I need You, Come, Sweet Spirit, I pray,
Come in Your strength and Your power, Come, in Your own gentle way.
© Gaither Music Co. Used by permission.

Assurance of Pardon

Trust In The Spirit

Pastoral Prayer	9:30 Mark Roberts	11:00 Jack Loo
Disciples' Prayer		

Anthem	*Where the Spirit of the Lord Is*	Steven Adams
	Cathedral Choir	

Joy In The Spirit

Sharing of the Joy   WITNESS: Mary Ellen Prichard

Tithes and Offerings

Offertory Solo	*Immortal, Invisible*	arr. John Rosasco
	Halbert Blair, Baritone	

*Doxology

*Prayer of Thanksgiving   9:30 Elder Richard Pepper   11:00 Elder J. Elder Bryan

*Hymn of Thanksgiving No. 147   *Spirit of God, Descend Upon My Heart*   MORECAMBE
Stanzas 1,4,5

Freedom Of The Spirit

Reading of the Word of God   II Corinthians 3:17-4:7

Prayer from the Word

Vision from the Word   Lloyd John Ogilvie

    Series: Here We Stand!

    Title: **The Fullness Of The Spirit**

    Text: *Now the Lord is the Spirit; and where the Spirit of the Lord is, there is liberty.*
    But we all, with unveiled face, beholding as in a mirror the glory of the Lord,
    are being transformed into the same image from glory to glory, just as by the
    Spirit of the Lord.   II Corinthians 3:17-18

         ...Be filled with the Spirit.   Ephesians 5:18

    Creed: **...I believe in the Holy Spirit...**

Life In The Spirit

Prayer of Dedication

Invitation

During and after the Hymn of Dedication, the Elders will be in the front of the Sanctuary to pray with and for you. Those who wish to receive Christ as Lord and Savior, those who desire prayer for spiritual, emotional and physical needs, those who need to commit their challenges and opportunities to the Lord for His guidance and intervening power, and those who are concerned about others are encouraged to come forward to kneel and pray.

*Hymn of Dedication No. 435   *The Savior Is Waiting*   CARMICHAEL

*Benediction

The congregation is requested to exit through the narthex rather than the doors at the front of the Sanctuary to facilitate the prayer ministry of the Elders at the steps of the chancel.

Playing of the Harold M. Ruddick Carillon

First Presbyterian Church of Hollywood

1760 North Gower Street · Hollywood, California 90028
Lloyd John Ogilvie, Senior Pastor · Phone: (213) 463-7161 · Valley (818)787-4651

MORNING WORSHIP · 9:30 & 11:00 a.m. · May 29, 1988

*Congregation will stand. · * * * Ushers will seat delayed worshipers.

As a courtesy to other worshipers, please use the rear doors
if you must leave before the service is over.

Hearing devices may be checked out from the Narthex prior to each service.
Please return them at the conclusion of the service.

Memorial Day Weekend
CELEBRATION OF WORSHIP

God Is Our Refuge And Strength

9:25 and 10:55	Silent Prayer	
Organ Prelude	*Andante* Kimo Smith, Organist	Felix Mendelssohn
Choral Adoration	*God is our Refuge and Strength* Cathedral Choir/Dr. Fred Bock, Director	Allan Pote
Prayer of Adoration	9:30 Dick Druary	11:00 Tod Bolsinger
***Hymn of Praise No. 687**	*God of Our Fathers*	NATIONAL HYMN

* * *

A Very Present Help In Trouble

Choral Call to Prayer	*I Must Tell Jesus* Cathedral Choir	Elisha H. Hoffman
Pastoral Prayer	9:30 Ralph Osborne	11:00 Jack Loo

Congregational Sung Response:

Hear our prayer, O Lord; hear our prayer, O Lord.
Incline Your ear to us, and grant us Your peace.

Anthem	*A Prayer* Cathedral Choir	William David Brown

Be with me, O Lord; lay before me Thy path of righteousness; allow me Thy
knowledge of truth, dear Lord. Thou art the Master and Saviour of all, dear
Lord. Save us from sin, dear Lord, we worship Thee. Comfort us with Thy
forgiveness, and teach us to love one another.

* * *

Therefore We Will Not Fear

Sharing of the Joy   Witness: Eunice Baumgardner

Tithes and Offerings

Offertory   *Awake, My Heart*   Jane Marshall
                              Cathedral Quartet
              Jan Payne, Lou Robbins, Jon Osbrink, Hal Blair

*Doxology   OLD HUNDREDTH

*Prayer of Thanksgiving   9:30 Elder Walter Gieselman   11:00 Elder Jim Coe

*Hymn of Preparation No. 387   *We Gather Together*   KREMSER
                              Stanzas 1, 2, & 3

The Lord Of Hosts Is With Us

Reading of the Word of God   Ephesians 6:10-12

Prayer for the Word

Vision from the Word   Lloyd John Ogilvie

   Series: Living The Disciples' Prayer
   Title: **The Neutralizer**
   Text: *And do not lead us into temptation, but deliver us from the evil one.*
      Matthew 6:13

      That you may bé able to stand against the wiles of the devil.
      Ephesians 6:11

Trust In The Lord

The Disciples' Prayer

Invitation

During and after the Hymn of Dedication, the Elders will be in the front of the Sanctuary to pray with and for you. Those who wish to receive Christ as Lord and Savior, those who desire prayer for spiritual, emotional and physical needs, those who need to commit their challenges and opportunities to the Lord for His guidance and intervening power, and those who are concerned about others are encouraged to come forward to kneel and pray.

*Hymn of Dedication No. 528   *God of Grace and God of Glory*   CWM RHONDDA

*Benediction

Playing of the Harold M. Ruddick Carillon

TONIGHT -- 6:30 p.m., Mears Center
Holy Communion
Dick Druary
Nursery Care Available

First Presbyterian Church of Hollywood

1760 North Gower Street   Hollywood, California 90028
Lloyd John Ogilvie, Senior Pastor   Phone: (213) 463-7161 Valley: (818) 787-4651

MORNING WORSHIP   **9:30 & 11:00 a.m.**   **JANUARY 24, 1988**

*Congregation will stand.   * * *Ushers will seat delayed worshipers.

As a courtesy to other worshipers, please use the rear doors if you must leave before the service is over.

Hearing devices may be checked out from the Narthex prior to each service.
Please return them at the conclusion of the service.

CELEBRATION OF WORSHIP
Rejoice In The Lord

9:25 and 10:55   Silent Prayer and Meditation

Choral Preparation for Worship:

> Surely the presence of the Lord is in this place,
> I can feel His mighty power and His grace.
> I can hear the brush of angels' wings,
> I see glory on each face;
> Surely the presence of the Lord is in this place.
> (Used by permission, Lanny Wolfe Music Co.)

Organ Prelude   *Jesu, Joy of Man's Desiring*   J. S. Bach
                              Kimo Smith, Organist

Choral Adoration   *Happy Are They Who Have God for Their Help*   Emma Lou Diemer
                        Cathedral Choir/Dr. Fred Bock, Director

Prayer of Adoration   9:30 Dick Druary   11:00 Lisa Andersen

*Hymn of Praise No. 377   *Joyful, Joyful We Adore Thee*   HYMN TO JOY
                             (Stanza 3 unaccompanied)

* * *

Experience His Grace

Choral Call to Prayer   *Fully Alive in His Presence*   William J. Gaither
                                  Cathedral Choir

Prayer of Confession

Congregational Sung Response:

> He touched me, O, He touched me,
> And O, the joy that floods my soul;
> Something happened, and now I know,
> He touched me and made me whole.
> (Used by permission, Gaither Music Co.)

Assurance of Pardon

Pastoral Prayer   9:30 Ralph Osborne   11:00 Jack Loo

Disciples' Prayer (sung)

* * *

Anthem	*Blessed Is the Man*	Jane Marshall
	Cathedral Choir	

Blessed is the man who walks not in the counsel of the ungodly, nor stands in the way of sinners, nor sits in the seat of scoffers; but his delight is in the law of the Lord, and on His law he meditates day and night. He is like a tree, planted by streams of water.

— from Psalm 1

Share His Joy

Sharing of the Joy	Witness: Gene Wohlberg	
Tithes and Offerings		
Offertory Solo	Jon Osbrink, Tenor	
***Doxology**		
***Prayer of Thanksgiving**	9:30 George Eastman	11:00 Jim Coe
***Hymn of Thanksgiving No. 78**	*My Hope Is in the Lord*	WAKEFIELD

Receive The Hope Of Happiness

Reading of the Word of God	Psalm 146:5; Jeremiah 17:7-8; Romans 12:12

Prayer from the Word

Hope from the Word	Lloyd John Ogilvie

Series: Where There's Hope, There's Life!

Title: **A Hope For Happiness**

Text: *Happy is he who has the God of Jacob for his help, whose hope is in the Lord his God.*
Psalm 146:5

Blessed is the man who trusts in the Lord, and whose hope is the Lord, for he shall be like a tree planted by the waters, which spreads out its roots by the river, and will not fear when heat comes, but her leaf will be green, and will not be anxious in the year of drought, nor will cease from yielding fruit.
Jeremiah 17:7-8

Rejoicing in hope, patient in tribulation, continuing steadfastly in prayer.
Romans 12:12

Spread His Hopeful Happiness

Prayer of Dedication

Invitation

During and after the Hymn of Dedication, the Elders will be in the front of the Sanctuary to pray with and for you. Those who wish to receive Christ as Lord and Savior, those who desire prayer for spiritual, emotional and physical needs, those who need to commit their challenges and opportunities to the Lord for His guidance and intervening power, and those who are concerned about others are encouraged to come forward to kneel and pray.

***Hymn of Dedication No. 468**	*Be Thou My Vision*	SLANE

Benediction

The congregation is requested to exit through the narthex rather than the doors at the front of the Sanctuary to facilitate the prayer ministry of the Elders at the steps of the chancel.

Playing of the Harold M. Ruddick Carillon

First Presbyterian Church of Hollywood

1760 North Gower Street   Hollywood, California 90028
Lloyd John Ogilvie, Senior Pastor   Phone: (213) 463-7161 Valley: (818) 787-4651

MORNING WORSHIP   9:30 & 11:00 a.m.   JANUARY 17, 1988

*Congregation will stand.   * * *Ushers will seat delayed worshipers.

As a courtesy to other worshipers, please use the rear doors if you must leave before the service is over.

Hearing devices may be checked out from the Narthex prior to each service.
Please return them at the conclusion of the service.

CELEBRATION OF WORSHIP

Goodness and Mercy

9:25 and 10:55	Silent Prayer and Meditation	
Organ Prelude	*Holy, Holy, Holy* Kimo Smith, Organist	Piet Post
Choral Adoration	*All That Hath Life and Breath* Cathedral Choir/Dr. Fred Bock, Director	René Clausen
Prayer of Adoration	9:30 George Henriksen	11:00 Jack Loo
***Hymn of Praise No. 323**	*Holy, Holy, Holy* Stanza 1: Men sing melody Stanza 2: Women sing melody Stanza 3: All sing parts Choral Interlude Stanza 4: All sing melody	NICAEA

* * *

Forgiveness and Love

Choral Call to Prayer	9:30 *Spirit of the Living God* 11:00 *He Giveth More Grace* Cathedral Choir	Daniel Iverson Hubert Mitchell
Pastoral Prayer	9:30 Dick Druary	11:00 Tod Bolsinger
Disciples' Prayer (sung)		

* * *

Anthem	*O Love, How Deep* Cathedral Choir	Everett Titcomb

O love, how deep, how broad, how high; how passing thought and fantasy, that God, the Son of God, should take our mortal form—for mortals' sake. For us He prayed, for us He taught, for us His daily works He wrought, by words and signs and actions, thus still seeking not Himself, but us. All glory to our Lord and God for love so deep, so high, so broad; the Trinity whom we adore forever and forevermore.

— Latin, 15th century

207

Grace and Gratitude

Sharing of the Joy

Tithes and Offerings

| **Offertory Solo** | *Jesus, the Very Thought of Thee* | Eric Thiman |
| | Lou Robbins, Contralto | |

*Doxology

| ***Prayer of Thanksgiving** | 9:30 Stan Kojac | 11:00 Jeffrey Jamison |

| ***Hymn of Thanksgiving No. 105** | *Grace Greater Than Our Sin* | MOODY |
| | (Stanzas 1 and 4 only) | |

Vision

| **Reading of the Word of God** | Romans 5:1-5 |

Prayer from the Word

| **Vision from the Word** | Lloyd John Ogilvie |

Series: Where There's Hope, There's Life!
Title: **Winning the Endurance Race**
Text: *And not only that, but we also glory in tribulations, knowing that tribulation produces perseverance; and perseverance, character; and character, hope. Now hope does not disappoint, because the love of God has been poured out in our hearts by the Holy Spirit who was given to us.* Romans 5:3-5

Dedication

Prayer of Dedication

Invitation
During and after the Hymn of Dedication, the Elders will be in the front of the Sanctuary to pray with and for you. Those who wish to receive Christ as Lord and Savior, those who desire prayer for spiritual, emotional and physical needs, those who need to commit their challenges and opportunities to the Lord for His guidance and intervening power, and those who are concerned about others are encouraged to come forward to kneel and pray.

| ***Hymn of Dedication No. 56** | *God Will Take Care of You* | GOD CARES |

Benediction

The congregation is requested to exit through the narthex rather than the doors at the front of the Sanctuary to facilitate the prayer ministry of the Elders at the steps of the chancel.

Playing of the Harold M. Ruddick Carillon